Therapy

(Looking and Listening to Myself, and Gaining Healing and Hope)

Stephanie Johnson-Rice

Therapy

Dedication

This book is dedicated to Rachel Lynn Ervin. You have been to me what many could have been and refused to be, for whatever reason. From the year 2007 until now, you have been the friend that has surpassed expectations! You are a shining jewel in the earth, but not everyone has seen your value. I do and I treasure you and will continue to enjoy your wealth and your glory—for you were created for a purpose that allowed me to be included! Thank you for all that you poured into my life. I thank God for having me reach out to you that day in Bruce Plastics in July of 2007! I love you beyond comprehension.

Proverbs 27:9
"A sweet friendship refreshes the soul."

Preface

This book was written during my personal healing process. I had held on to so many things for years, and it was causing me to suffer in my daily living. I never knew how serious it was until I began writing this and the wounds began to heal within me. I was living a life that looked so very successful on the outside. I was preaching and doing poetry and holding workshops and seeing others healed and delivered and I was still bound. After writing this, I could see so much more clearly. And I am a different individual because of the situations I verbally vomited onto paper. I am now thriving instead of surviving. And the process is ongoing. Be set free!

Misunderstood

"Lord, you have examined me, and you know me. You know everything I do; from far away you understand all my thoughts. You see me, whether I am working or resting; you know all my actions…Your knowledge of me is too deep; it is beyond my understanding."

Psalm 139:1, 3, 6

"Being misunderstood by the people whose opinions you value is absolutely the most painful."

Gloria Steinem

I sucker punched my mother in her face earlier this month. Now it sounds harsh, but it was because I loved her. It sounds paradoxical, I know. But if I didn't love her so much, I would not have been so angry with her. "Be angry, and yet do not sin; do not let the sun go down on your anger." (Ephesians 4:26) Unfortunately, I carried anger with me for years, and it became a part of my every makeup. And on that day, I exploded. Ugh!!! It was awful! I felt as though I had been trying to get her to love me, trying to do everything I could to make her proud of me, but it just wasn't to be. I wish that you could read both sides of this story, but all I have is mine. And maybe I am looking through eyes that aren't experiencing clear vision. I just wish that things had been different in my childhood and my upbringing. Now don't get anything twisted: this isn't to bash her. My story, like I said, is my story. If you don't know her and can't speak on it, then you really don't know anyway. But some do...and that is a small satisfaction, for at times I thought that I was stone crazy. She is spoken well of in various circles, and this is just fine with me. I am glad that she has support and much love given to her. I can accept the fact that she is loved. I just find it difficult to deal with the issue of her not loving me. She says she does. But actions carry more weight. And they speak much more loudly! In different circles, my name is spoken of in different ways. Some love me—others, not so much. I can tell by the reaction when I walk up how some feel about me—they don't even realize that their faces tell me the entire story. And I used to be petty and make them speak to me and hug me, knowing that they couldn't stand me. Now, though, I don't waste my good time and energy. I speak and keep it moving. Your reaction, your response is of no importance to me. I wish that I could say that about my mother. I wish that I could say that it didn't bother me how she differentiated between me and the others. I wish that I could say that she had my back and I had hers, no matter what. All these wishes...and no genie to come up out the lamp to make them come true. I tried to speak with her face to face about so many things and maybe I was just asking too much of her. Maybe she didn't recognize the toxicity that she brought to the table with us? I don't believe that is true, but I am trying to give the benefit of the doubt. I was the cause of many of the messes that occurred, especially with my daddy, and he didn't deserve that. He was the real MVP. I mean, if you are the father of kids that aren't yours biologically, but you stayed and took care of them as if they were your own without reservation, then you are going above and beyond. I didn't treat him well enough. I didn't spend enough time with him. I don't know if he knew that he was important to me and how this life doesn't shine as brightly since he left this earth. It's darker now. I didn't appreciate him like I should have. I know that he now is with his grandchildren and smiling. I am grateful to know that he is at peace.

Finally Free

"You, my brothers and sisters, were called to be free."
Galatians 5:13

"Nobody can give you freedom…you take it."   Malcolm X

I am just now beginning to experience complete freedom. I know that sounds crazy—even to me because I am 48-years-old. But I have been a prisoner to so many different things and so many different people, that I was trapped, held captive, and all the time I was still smiling. It is amazing what can be hidden behind a beautiful smile. Sometimes I felt that my small frame wasn't going to support all the frustration and the pain. I was afraid that I was going to snap on some people, some deserving and some innocent! I would feel the weight of the load that I was carrying; I would speak to myself under my breath, encouraging myself, because all I wanted to do was to go in my room, close the door, climb in my bed and retreat into a depression-filled coma. Sleeping brings peace to me. During one phase of my life, I was constantly fighting in my sleep, as others were trying to kill me by stabbing or shooting me. And I am deranged enough to fight back, whether asleep or awake, so often I would awaken to my husband grabbing my arms or shaking me awake. It was worse when I was enduring the nightmares, too, because that meant no peace, whether I was awake or asleep. I ended up tired and edgy, and that was dangerous to me and everyone else. Fatigue had me snapping at any little thing that irritated me.

It is difficult for me to remember the good times in my life, the times where I was happy and worry-free. I am sure that there had to be some. But my recollections of them are few. Maybe because I have repressed so much of my life in order to maintain my sanity. If I replayed the mess that was my life, I would have committed suicide—and I was planning on doing that the very night that God decided to speak to me and asked me to try Him. I had tried everything else. Nothing satisfied. I was still unhappy and seeking something to fill the void inside. But you know what? After receiving Him, all hell broke loose! I was confused. Wasn't giving my life to Christ supposed to even out the trials in my life? I was told that by some misguided Christian whom God will not allow me to remember. I would love to go have a little talk with them about the great big lie that they fed me! I thought I was seriously doing wrong because everything fell apart! But it is the greatest decision that I have ever made, and after so many backslidden occurrences in which He still never left me and continually let me know it, I finally told Him that He was forever stuck with me. His love will win you over, I tell you. I remember running from Him and feeling Him at my neck, if you understand what I'm saying! He was determined to have me, and it felt good to be wanted! All my life I had read the Bible, and I thought it a book of fairy tales. I didn't see any of the signs and wonders occurring that I was reading about and so I didn't think it could really be true. My life was in shambles and I was angry and would literally curse Him—and He still sought after me! Unconditional love—there is nothing like it! I have basked in it and will forever love Him! God loves everyone—EVERYONE!! Stop acting like He didn't die for the murderer, pedophile, rapist, and any other sinner we think is beyond the grasp of the Savior! The Blood still works! Y'all get on my sanctified nerve, thinking that the perpetrator doesn't need prayer like the victim does! They did the act—they might need more!! We will talk about people but never lift them up in prayer. And you are useless. Yeah, I said it. "Be a doer of His Word and not a hearer only," says James 1:22. The Church members are the main ones who are doing the shaming. The very ones proclaiming Him are the ones who are not representing Him! It is sad, but true. And of course, I don't mean everyone in the Church. There are genuine individuals seeking His life and living the kingdom mandate of bringing Heaven to Earth. But others are making excuses and living the way they choose and thinking it is ok. That's deceit. You're deceived. But don't let me stop you—the Holy Spirit will convict those who are His.

Wounded Woman

"My wounds grow foul and fester because of my folly."
Psalm 38:5

"To heal a wound, you need to stop touching it."

I am a 48-year-old woman going through the healing stages of hurt that originated in my childhood and sometimes I am tired of even talking about it. That is what has gotten me to this point in the first place, keeping it all inside. My inability to trust those around me because trust just wasn't something I had or was freely given. I was overlooked, ignored, and disregarded. Therefore, I felt as though I was nothing, nobody. Then people began to call upon me for the gifts/talents that they saw in my life and I wasn't able to see that they didn't care for me at all; they were just using me for their own purposes. Some individuals only spoke to me to extend the invitation but refused to acknowledge me once I arrived at the venue to do whatever was asked of me. I was even more confused and disappointed. I feel as though depression has held my hand throughout most of my life, being more of a constant friend than Jesus! At that time, I did not know that Jesus was really real. The Bible I was reading was too much for me to believe that it actually happened. It was full of people who did great things, but I wasn't seeing that played out in my reality. I want people to know that, yes, God gets all the glory. But if you were not a willing instrument in doing His work, no one can see that He is real!! No one can see that He exists! Obedience is the best evidence, I tell you! To see someone walk in their purpose—that's powerful! Many are trying to get into some title or some calling, and we are needing purposeful people! The glory of God shines through the ones doing exactly what they were called to do! (Instead of those who are trying to be called this title or that title—stop playing!) God calls us by our names. I didn't want to be called anything. I was called to evangelize and was running so hard; I should have pulled spiritual muscles! I didn't think I was worthy. If I could not win the love of my own mother, how could this perfect being, this perfect God single me out for anything? I tried to tell Him that He was mistaken. There were others who were more qualified. I went to one ministry and no matter how many times I attended, the prophetess would look me directly in the face and say, "God is tired of you! He doesn't want a perfect vessel; He wants a willing vessel! People are dying and their blood is on your hands!" And I would just cry, thinking, "She doesn't know how badly I have treated Him! I have cursed Him! I am not a good choice!" That's not the uplifting word that so many seek to get from the prophet! But I tell you what, it got me thinking! A willing vessel instead of a perfect vessel? Yes, I could be that. I could list all my flaws. I could list everything wrong with me! It was harder for me to give you positive qualities! I felt so low! But God sees us for who we really are! (I'm smiling even as I typed that last sentence!) The potential that we have in Him is limitless!

We are truly supernatural! We can accomplish things through Him that we never dared to dream! I am still in awe of the things that He has done in my life and I am so grateful! He had to work through a broken soul, with a broken heart. But He triumphed!

Unreciprocated

"So in everything, do to others what you would have them do to you, for this sums up the Law and the Prophets."
                    Matthew 7:12 (NIV)

"Sometimes you have to give up on people. Not because you don't care, but because they don't."

I used to always wonder why I could support an event or program over and over again, but when it was time for one of my events...there were crickets and katydids from the very ones whom I had so eagerly supported. Now I am not talking about every individual, because I know that many of the people I networked with were as busy, if not busier, than I was. But I am speaking of the ones who repeatedly called upon me but did not deem it necessary to show their faces on my behalf. I heard one of my spiritual sisters call it "pimpin' my purpose"! You were using me to get what I had, knowing that people were going to come and appreciate it! I was a fool for a long time, baby...but this is the end. With freedom comes this special attitude that will let you know that there will be no more playing with me or my God-given gifts! It was like being in a relationship where you swear the man will change, but he and the spectators are laughing at your expense. But my crooked teeth are on display now, boo! I'm chuckling and guffawing and knee-slapping! I have the joy that comes with releasing the people and the pain I acquired from them! I didn't sign up for this and I won't be manning that table! I've got all this and use it when it is genuinely treasured. So you can stop with the text messages and inboxes, because I am not even responding. Shoot, I probably won't even read them!

Now, please excuse me if I sound a little angry and quite frustrated. I admit it, yes, I am. But this book is helping me to heal. I am using my laptop as my therapist. And it is feeling mighty good. I am not being judged while I vomit my inner feelings upon this paper, and you always feel better after vomiting...or I do anyway. So, while the contents of this book are filthy and unbecoming, I am becoming more beautiful as I release my emotions and begin to heal. Some of you know what I mean.

Usually we hold in the things we are dealing with, due to our not being able to trust the ones we are speaking with. I have had family members tell my personal business to others, best friends revealing secrets I have told them in confidence...so I begin to literally have a dialogue with myself. Crazy? No, it was a necessity! I could trust me, so I unloaded what I was dealing with, and then I encouraged myself, because others were failing me, and I was done. It got so rough at one point that I was depressed at hearing the trials that I was going through, and I had to pray for myself as if I weren't myself! It sounds funny to me now, but at that moment, I was in crisis. God did not make man to be alone, but most of us are battling things and are unable to share it with another soul. This is not the way it is intended to be. And I know that the various ailments and aches in my body were occurring due to the tension and anxiety and worry that I was carrying within me.

I think back often to when I lived in Colony Park, and I was so happy. That memory both makes me happy and makes me sad, because I miss that woman. She was handling her business and taking care of her son and she remembers his joy of living and her satisfaction with life. It has been a long time since I have felt that. This should not be. I am miserable and am fighting a war that seems to be taking everything that I have, both physically and emotionally. There are times when I am up all night and don't fall asleep until the morning comes as I replay the mistakes in my mind until a migraine comes to keep me company. How could I be so old and not have accomplished the basics? I own no car and no home. I am unemployed and not having the income coming in is weighing me down. I cannot stand to be fully dependent on anyone else unless it is God Himself. But I will give praise for the people that He has placed in my life during this crazy time, after I was whining about the people that He was cutting off! He is amazing in how He works. The people I am surrounded by now are truly God sent and I am grateful!

Parenthood

8 Listen, my son, to your father's instruction and do not forsake your mother's teaching.
9 They are a garland to grace your head and a chain to adorn your neck.

Proverbs 1:8-9

"Everybody knows how to raise children, except the people who have them."

P.J. O'Rourke

I found out that my father wasn't really my father. I am not proud of the way that I treated him once that was relayed to me. I was disrespectful and mean and he didn't deserve that. One of my sisters told me that he found out years later and cried. I have been dealing with that ever since she said it. But he knew that I loved him--we had become closer in my adult years. I apologized to him, and he stated that he didn't even think about the past anymore and he forgave me. I wish I had spent more time with him, of course; he is now gone and hindsight is 20/20. I hate that I didn't have the good sense to learn from him, especially about money and how to save it, and how to keep my temper under control and how to relax and enjoy fishing. I try to honor him now, but nothing is the same. I still post pics of him and me--it is a pic where I am little. It is my very favorite. I lost the one where he had his arm around me when I was about to graduate from high school. You get to a place where you appreciate the small things, especially when you lose someone, and regret speaks to you like a lover. I remember the laughter though. He was always somewhere making somebody laugh. I don't even know the pain he endured, because very few saw that side.

And those are the friends that you need to check on--check on the friends who are continually making sure that others are good and striving to put a smile on their faces. I now hear in my head when he would say, "Step, y'all gotta check on me, because I could die in here in this trailer, and no one would know." He was simply asking to be shown a little love, a little concern. I failed at showing him how much I love him. It is too late now but knowing that he is in Heaven with Zachary and Derrell makes me feel so much better. Zachary and Derrell are my nephews who died in a house fire about a month before my son Stephano was born. He is named after them. So it gives me great pleasure to know that he doesn't ever have to worry anymore.

I knew who my biological father was, and he knew who I was. I rarely saw him, so I didn't know him well. I know he had two other children (and eventually another, whom I only found out about recently.) I didn't tell a lot of people about what was going on--this was too complicated! But I have been in touch with my sisters after receiving a phone call one afternoon, and I realized that the others knew of my relationship to them. I thank God for my sisters reaching out to me. I wish that we could have had a closer relationship sooner and gotten to know each other better. It is difficult for me to have close relationships now, unless you move in the arena I am networking in. But my biological father died last year...I never knew what he thought of me or the circumstances. I hold no animosity or anything towards anyone. It is what it is.

Deafness

"But I, like a deaf man, do not hear; and I am like a mute man who does not open his mouth."
Psalm 38:13

"No one is as deaf as the man who will not listen."
Jewish Proverb

Recently I have stopped talking as much...since it seems as if I am disregarded and ignored. I know exactly what I'm talking about, but when it is dealing with others, they pay me no attention. It used to be that I would speak the knowledge, then they would pay me no attention, but after a crisis hit, then they would return to me and I would help them fix it. When I realized how stupid I was for helping people who wouldn't regard my suggestions in the first place, I put a stop to that. If I'm not good enough to listen to initially, then I am not good enough to help you take care of your mess. Looking back on how idiotic I was and how they probably laughed at me used to make me angry. Now I just sit and pray because I know that I was the answer for a number of people when it came to their lives. That sounds like bragging, but it is not. I know my importance. I know what I bring to the table. I know how valuable I am. God has gifted me with numerous skills and I have perfected them to where they shine like gold! I am no longer speaking so much. I have very little to say after realizing what was happening. But it's a good thing. I should have done this long ago. You know that I have something you need, otherwise you wouldn't come to me in the first place. But to come and then brush me aside? No, thank you. I have better things to do. I have people who know my worth. I have other assignments to complete. It hurts me, but I will be okay. Everything will be alright. I always come out on top. I have the Lord on my side, and He is the One Who will sustain me through it all. I try not to rejoice in the fact that many times I see them when they fall on their faces...it truly isn't a joyful experience for me, but I want to go to them and say, "I told you so! You didn't want to listen!" I get angry when the answer is placed before them, but they chose a different, unproductive path. I am made to feel like nothing, when you came to me for something. It amazes me how ignorant and uncaring humanity can be.

Depression

"But you, LORD, are a shield around me, my glory, the One who lifts my head high."

Psalm 3:3

"You know you're having a bad day when even the Rice Krispies give you silent treatment."

People are surprised to hear that I battle depression sometimes. It doesn't show--I am always on the go, at some event, helping somebody do something. But the hardest times are in the early morning hours, before bed, or just waking up. I literally have to drag myself out of bed and speak over myself just to get started. Now, once I get into motion, it becomes a little better. But getting into motion...that's the key. I don't know why people feel as though I don't have any battles, that I'm not fighting some wars...I want you to know that when you are walking in your purpose and trying to please God on purpose, you will be fought!! And the fight will be fierce!! The enemy does not like the fact that you are going forth and advancing the Kingdom! I remember one prophetess telling me, "The devil hates when you wake up in the morning!" Wow!! Thank God for my obedience! I want the world to see Jesus in me! I want the life of Jesus to flow through me! But it isn't easy! Obedience brings blessings but it also brings warfare! So you need to know the Word of God and the weapons you have been given and you need to be spiritually clothed in the armor in order to be victorious! I can tell you, depression can be overcome! And it will check back with you to see what you are going to do. I have been successful on some days and unsuccessful on the rest. I am not saying that I win every time, and when I lose, it is my fault! He has given me all things pertaining to life and godliness. I am already an overcomer in the spirit--I just have to walk it out in the natural.

Unworthy

"But the centurion said, "Lord, I am not worthy for You to come under my roof, but just say the word, and my servant will be healed."

Matthew 8:8

You are very powerful, provided you know how powerful you are.
— Yogi Bahaman

There are moments when I am in the midst of worshipping God and I feel unworthy to even be where I am. I know it can be the enemy playing with my mind, but let's just be realistic: often it is Stephanie playing mind games with Stephanie. I am in a place where I have never been before. I know who I am and exactly what I have been placed on this earth to do. Yet there are instances where I feel unworthy. I remember who I used to be and what I used to do; I recall what I used to say and how I used to act. And it only encourages me. What do I mean, you say? How does the feeling of unworthiness contribute to my being encouraged? Because I know that Satan is only trying to get me to recollect the foolishness that I used to do as a result of his being aware of who I am now and more importantly, what I am about to do! I don't know how he is even aware of these good things coming my way, but he can't stand it and he is determined to make me stumble and fall! I look back on where I have come from and can only praise the Lord for the things that He has done and the ways that He has made and how He has given me beauty for ashes! He makes me look beautiful in spite of all the mess I have been through! He shows Himself strong on my behalf and has me winning every battle if I only obey Him and follow His principles! Unworthy? It followed me from childhood and tried to take hold of me to keep me from progressing into the new life awaiting me both here and now, and in the afterlife, when I live again! Victory is so sweet!

Not Guilty

"There is therefore now no condemnation for those who are in Christ Jesus."

Romans 8:1

"Any fool can criticize, complain, and condemn—and most fools do. But it takes character and self-control to be understanding and forgiving."
— Dale Carnegie, How to Win Friends and Influence People

I went to court today for assault and battery 3rd degree. I had pled guilty after the judge explained it all to me, looking as if he were bored--but probably just used to going through the motions. I can't imagine giving that speech day in and day out, over and over again at each trial. Then the officer that arrested me told the judge that my mother was wanting to drop the charges. I didn't know what to think...we were in the midst of the proceedings! But the judge stamped the paperwork and said they found Stephanie Johnson-Rice not guilty. I left confused, but I was so glad. I was wondering what the cause was, but I wasn't going to contact her to ask. Maybe I will hear it through the grapevine. Because if I got to the point where I hit her, then I believe I need to stay away. I felt badly for her, because she was there all alone. I don't know what is going on in her mind. I pray that she is at peace. I finally have mine. Do people not realize what you do for them, what you are for them, until it's something happening that separates you? I am in a place now where I am alone most of the time when not conducting business--Kingdom business. You are made aware of so much when you are alone with your thoughts. But I am happier at this time. I know the Lord warned me that He was going to cut off some people...but it was drastic! I am grateful, though, even if it was some of the ones I never expected to be separated from. He knows what He is doing. I just have to trust him. And as easy as it sounds--sometimes that is the hardest part, especially for someone who likes to know what's going on and be in control.

Burden-Bearer

"Cast your burden on the Lord, and He shall sustain you; He shall never permit the righteous to be moved"

Psalm 55:22

"I didn't want to upset my loved ones, but I couldn't carry this alone."

— Julie Flygare, Wide Awake and Dreaming: A Memoir

It is one gift that I have spiritually that I often wish I didn't. It is what the people in the world would call an "empath." I can feel the feelings of others and it's as if I'm going through it myself. I feel like crying or raging or going into the room and closing myself off from the world. I can awaken with the joy of the Lord but get around an individual and immediately am overwhelmed with their emotions. I pray that they are experiencing some sort of relief with my helping to bear their burdens, because if I am weighted down, then who knows how much they are dealing with. And to think that God took on all our sins and infirmities and weaknesses upon Himself upon the cross, while He was experiencing such excruciating pain from the crucifixion! I had read recently about all the pains He dealt with--that part isn't always preached or taught. The love He has for us--the things He has done for us! His love is beyond what we can even imagine!! And it shames me to say that I complain about the smallest test or trial! Ugh!! I have got to be a better, stronger soldier. I have got to endure hardness as a good soldier of Christ Jesus. I realize that I have been a whiny Christian most my life! Just calling it venting or talking to a close friend, when it is low key whining and crying. The Lord reveals to me the things I need to work on, and whew! That one really got me! Big baby!! Yeah, I said it to myself! Grow up!! Stand firm! He has got you and you got this! Forward!! Advance the Kingdom!

Self-Esteem

"But blessed is the one who trusts in the Lord,
  whose confidence is in him."
Jeremiah 17:7

"You yourself, as much as anybody in the entire universe, deserve your love and affection."
– Buddha

I didn't have high self-esteem. I was one who had students talking about me and my clothes right to my face. They weren't ashamed to do it; they were proud and mocking. And I sat there and allowed them to demean me, with smirks and laughter. I quietly sat and endured, for I believed that I was whatever they said I was: ugly, stupid, whatever...it didn't matter. It is still an ongoing battle even now. I was just given a prophecy that stated that I would be one of the greatest preachers in this area and that I needed to stop questioning God asking Him, "Why me? I have done so much wrong." This confirmed the word given to one of my close Christian brothers, who texted me that very message. It is difficult for me to hear a good prophecy and accept it as being for me because the first thing I do is question myself and God. I swear that there are more qualified candidates! I list my flaws and suggest the other recipients that I would deem more qualified for Him! I would recommend that anyone who has children begin to instill in them healthy self-esteem. Let them know that they are beautiful, loved, talented, intelligent, etc. When this is done, it is not as easy for someone to come in and break them down emotionally and mentally. They will have already been built up into strong individuals. When my son was born, I continually spoke to him, telling him that he was someone of worth, that he was handsome; he was smart, etc. So when given a compliment, he would say, "I know! My mama told me!" And I had to then let him know that the acceptable thing to say is, "Thank you." But I was successful in my affirming him from birth! I am proud of him. He is a young man who doesn't care about looks, money, clothes, etc. He is just who he is and what you do, say, wear, think--all that doesn't faze him. He will be just as cool with the janitor as with the CEO because he looks at everyone equally, and expects the same. Affirm your children. Affirm your friends. Affirm your spouse. Just be the doggone best you can be to anyone you come into contact with. Be a human being!

Molestation

"Come to me, all you who are weary and burdened, and I will give you rest. Take my yoke upon you and learn from me, for I am gentle and humble in heart, and you will find rest for your souls. For my yoke is easy and my burden is light"
Matthew 11:28-30

"Child abuse casts a shadow the length of a lifetime."
Herbert Ward

I don't speak on molestation much. It happened but it didn't cripple me, if you understand what I'm saying. I have heard testimony of how it turned some towards promiscuity and others towards celibacy or homosexuality. I am indifferent, it seems to me. I became promiscuous because I was looking for the love I felt I lacked in my life. But even in the midst of the very act, I knew this dude didn't care about me. And the one who did care about me later on in life was someone else's husband, and you know how that turned out. The mistress usually doesn't win the man. So I was not blind to what was going to happen with that relationship. I was determined to make sure that I did all I could to ensure that my son was not molested--I wanted his life to be better than mine. I thank God that he speaks of his childhood with happiness. I hated mine. You would think that I would have allowed the molestation to continue, especially since I was looking for someone to show me any kind of affection. Sounds crazy, but I needed to know that someone saw me. I mean really SAW me. It felt as if I were overlooked unless needed for something, not valued just because it was me. I had to give something or do something for me to be treasured, but that wasn't even lasting. I don't talk about being molested, because I don't feel like it was something that affected my life in a great way. It happened. I was disturbed about it, enough to tell my mother. She laughed. I went to my room in confusion. Then she told me to tell the mother of the one who molested me. I did. She turned from me and said she didn't want to hear it, and left the room. I know it is hard to deal with, and I am sure hearing it was not easy. But I am free from any wounds that it caused; you know that God is such a faithful Healer!

Friends

"Walk with the wise and become wise, for a companion of fools suffers harm."

Proverbs 13:20

"Never let your best friends get lonely…keep disturbing them."

I went to one of my friend's weddings today. I don't generally do weddings, but this chick is special to me, and I didn't hesitate to say yes when I received her invitation. She is one soul who will give you the shirt off her back! I have loved her since forever! We have always been there for each other, even if we don't talk every day--and I don't talk every day to anybody, to tell the truth. My people know how I feel about them. I am not the one to stay in touch daily; who knows when you will hear from me, but I do need to get better at keeping in touch. She wore a beautiful black dress with red Converse tennis shoes! I was in awe at how smashing she looked when I saw her all dolled up! I hate that the wedding preparations are so stressful, but in the end, it was all worth it! I watched as friends and family took the time to love on her, especially her children. I was taking photos and I captured moments of them loving their mother in their own special way. I want her to know that she is special to me. I want her to feel the love that I have for her and know that she has a compartment in my heart. I am willing to do whatever I can to express my affection.

My parting words to her was that no matter what happened, no matter if she or I were to go by the grave or until the Rapture, that I love her dearly and hope she knows it. And I am aware that she does, but it does a heart good to hear it. I was honored to be asked to share in her special day, and I pray that I was a blessing to her. I told her that I wasn't working, so that I would get her a gift later, and she looked at me and said, "You are the gift!" And my soul sang. It is my desire to make those around me feel treasured. At least with her, I have achieved that goal. I like how she is her genuine self around me, no frills, no facades, no faces. That is one characteristic that drew me to her. It doesn't matter who you are; we all get the same person. That seems to be rare nowadays. She is the real deal.

Poetry

"We have become his poetry, a re-created people that will fulfill the destiny he has given each of us, for we are joined to Jesus, the Anointed One. Even before we were born, God planned in advance *our destiny* and the good works we would do *to fulfill it*!"
Ephesians 2:10

"If you cannot be the poet, be the poem."

Poetry is such a therapeutic art. I take whatever I am feeling within me and write it down, transferring it from my heart onto a sheet of paper, weighing it down with me. I place the heartache and voice my agony in a line that may or may not rhyme. Because my life isn't always soothing and symphonic. So coming forth violently from my soul are torrents of letters dancing into words and sentences and paragraphs ending in a period. I catch myself when I read myself. I know myself and I listen to myself. Sometimes I hear myself and cringe--I am so country!! But I love her as well as battle her. The rhythm lulls me into a creative creature that demands that you stop and hear the wind exiting my lungs. I stand in a waterfall of words that drench me and dress me in artistic attire. I am honored to be one that is in love with words, one who feels fully satisfied to partake of a poem that displays word play that is more engaging than two star struck lovers. When I hear the melodic sound of spoken word by a creative creation that the Creator has brought forth from dust and divinity, I smile. We are put on earth to bring forth the glory of the Lord down from Heaven, and the poet has been sprinkled with just a little smidgen of angelic, anointed, almighty artistry. I often put you on the pages of a poem, spitting out the impression that you may have left on me, be it good, bad, or ugly. In the words of a poem, I lose whatever I had held onto and allow freedom to chase me, instead of my seeking it and it eluding me. I slip from the chains that try to link my soul with sewage and dance determinedly with words that lift me beyond where I stand in the natural realm. Poetry is the verbiage of my peace.

Unexpected Blessings

"May God bless us still, so that all the ends of the earth will fear Him."

Psalm 67:7

"I think in every lesson, there is a blessing…"
Alonzo Mourning

There are days when it takes everything in me just to get out of bed and go forth in my purpose. Today was a day when I woke up early to get on the Arise Ministries prayer line. I am not a morning person, but I set the alarm and decided to join in. It took a lot of discipline to awaken...I had not slept well, and the lazy part of me told me to go back to sleep and try again the next morning. I didn't listen to me, and I dialed the number and waited. I sat silently in agreement as the prayer went forth and I felt better when it was done. I lay there until I drifted back off to sleep. When I started the day, it was sort of hectic, and I was frazzled; but determined to have a good day. I fellowshipped with some fellow artists over breakfast, enjoying the company of those who know the good, bad, and ugly and still love and encourage you! I am grateful for the ones God has placed in my life strategically. There are some for every aspect of my life, and I don't take them for granted. As Paul said in his epistle, "I thank my God every time I think of you!" I try to show the people in my life that I am appreciative of them and their friendships. I hope my love can be felt.

My hair was a flaming hot mess! My baby sister walked in the house, and asked me, "What's going on with that?" I told her it needed to be done, but since I was not working, I didn't have the money. She immediately snatched me up, took me to the hair store, paid for my hair, then did it for me!! I hadn't even asked!! I wasn't even expecting it! God knows!

Something as simple as a brand-new hairdo was a huge blessing to me! I have been in the mirror telling myself how cute I am! God is faithful!

Motherhood

"Children, obey your parents in the Lord, for this is right.
2 "Honor your father and mother"—which is the first
commandment with a promise—
3 "so that it may go well with you and that you may enjoy long life
on the earth."

Ephesians 6:1-3

"Nobody loves me but my mother, and she could be jivin' too."
B. B. King

I did not think that I would be a good mother. I was the oldest of five girls, and I had to help out with my younger sisters. I was not a willing participant! I told my mother, "You had these kids; I didn't!" I felt as though I would be resentful of the child, as I had become with my sisters, who were in the middle of a mess that they didn't ask for. Mama told me to take care of them; I did so with hostility and anger. Who knows what these poor babies were thinking? As they got older, they would lie on me and get me into trouble. I laughed with one sister as she remembered doing so--we were watching TV, and she calmly got up, went to the back where Mama was, and said, "Stephanie hit me." *What the what???!!* I got into trouble, because Mama believed her. I was an angry child, so it made sense that Mama would believe her. Because I was miserable, so I was going to make sure that everyone else was just as miserable! I would wake up mad, so I went on a rampage, just looking for a fight. Those poor kids...having to deal with this crazy chick everyday...that must have been so difficult, never knowing when I would have another tantrum. I am glad that we all became closer after we got older. Lord knows I would understand if they never spoke to me again. I can be something else, chile...something ugly!

 So, I felt that I wasn't good enough to be a mother. I got pregnant and was literally depressed. I really felt for the kid--it was going to have to deal with me. But my son Stephano Derrell Arnez Johnson is the greatest accomplishment of my life! He helped to save my life, because he was, and still is, such a comedian! He doesn't even realize how funny he is. I cannot go anywhere without someone asking me about him and telling me how proud they are of him. Sometimes he asks me why they are proud of him--he just doesn't realize who he is and what he has done. He is amazing! He thinks that I say that because I am his mother...no, sir, I speak the truth! He is a young man with intelligence, compassion, and so many gifts. I am proud to be his mom. He made motherhood easy. He helped me by being my own personal comedian. God knew exactly what He was doing when He sent that child to me! I love that kid!

Integrity

"The integrity of the upright guides them, but the unfaithful are destroyed by their duplicity."

Proverbs 11:3

"It is true that integrity alone won't make you a leader, but without integrity you will never be one."

Zig Ziar

Most Christians that I come in contact with are some of the whiniest, dirtiest, weakest people on the planet! I am beyond trying to understand people anymore...the ones that are supposed to uphold a standard are the very ones lowering it with their actions! Now I am nobody's perfect gift, but I am also one to let you know that I was wrong. I keep encountering believers who will do things I have done but will not own up to it! All the excuses that come up from their mouths which do not excuse what you have done. It amazes me how we as the born-again Christian acts like the long life sinner and think nothing of it! This is why the world scoffs at our titles, services and words. Because we have no integrity; our words do not line up with His Word and our actions definitely show us to be against the Word instead of lined up with the Word. I have had people approach me regarding something that I have said or done...and I'm initially shocked because they have already done the very same to me and I forgave and let it slide, but they come to me as if they were never in the wrong! I miss being able to pop off vocally like I did before I was saved...I got so much off my chest and walked off with a smile on my face. But that's not God. And if I love Him, then I will honor and keep His commandments. I desire to please Him. I notice that Christians want to be treated a certain way, but do not feel obligated to reciprocate. You are wrong. I was afraid in the beginning when God first began removing people from my life, because I don't have a large circle of friends as it is. I network with many, but that's Kingdom business. The majority of the people you see me with, I cannot count on when the chips are down. That's saddening. But I have endured some things that allow me to just keep it moving, head up, even when I have cried tears in the background. Don't get it twisted--I shall prevail!!!

Self-Evaluation

"Therefore, my dear friends, as you have always obeyed--not only in my presence, but now much more in my absence--continue to work out your salvation with fear and trembling,"
Philippians 2:12

"Courage doesn't happen when you have all the answers. It happens when you are ready to face the questions you have been avoiding your whole life."
Shannon L. Alder

I do a lot. God has given me many gifts. But I am the crazy one that evaluates my performance and gives myself an F!! I can get a standing ovation, but I will get home by myself and tear my poem/sermon/hosting apart bit by bit, saying, "I didn't do this or that." I am asked to do different things at many workshops, events, and ministries, but I will beat myself up for weeks if I think that I didn't do well enough. I notice that I will focus on one mistake that I made years ago and beat myself up--and it has been 15 years ago!! I am not sure where this is coming from...I get a lot of positive feedback and encouragement from those in my circle. There is no reason for me to be doing this to Stephanie. I can do 99 things perfectly, but I will focus on the 1 thing that I messed up on! This is madness. This is anxiety and I didn't even know this until I read a meme on Facebook! What is going on? I love how I dress and speak and preach and teach, but every time I do, I'm critiquing and criticizing, tearing myself down. This must be dealt with. I could get into an argument with someone; it could be their fault, but I will get home and say, "Stephanie, you were wrong for that" even though my mouth is declaring that they were wrong. You never know what someone is dealing with, because most people don't see this part of me. Sometimes I will speak things over with my son, but I don't discuss this with him on a regular basis. I must deal with it; I will prevail over it. I speak positive affirmations over her throughout the day. I will see myself as God sees me, and I will continue to shine like a jewel in His land!

Un-rooted

"Let your roots grow down into him, and let your lives be built on him. Then your faith will grow strong in the truth you were taught, and you will overflow with thankfulness."
Colossians 2:7

"To move freely, one must be deeply rooted."

I wish that I had been like my father, remaining on a job for years. I was one who would leave if I wasn't satisfied with what was going on, not realizing that I was causing my work history to look bad. It wasn't as if I couldn't get a job; it was easy to get a job, but I should have picked a job and remained--getting the 401K and all the perks that came with longevity. I think back on how Daddy worked at Glen Raven for years...how good a worker he was...how people spoke well of him. I job-hopped for years. Come to think of it, I even church-hopped, though I stayed at churches longer than I did at jobs! I would leave churches all out of order, not scheduling a meeting with the pastor to talk about my decision, maybe they would get an email. Thank God that is in the past. I am more mature now and can voice my opinions and talk about what's going on instead of just getting angry and leaving. I was feeling as though I wasn't being heard and so my absence would be more effective. In some cases, it was, but it still wasn't the right decision to make. Looking back on life, you can see the wrongs so clearly. In that moment, where I felt like I was worthless because my voice wasn't being heard, I took immediate action. But I didn't look at anything from the opposite side--maybe they couldn't do what I was asking, or maybe not at that time, or maybe it was not even a good idea that I was proposing. But I could have talked more and did less until I knew the facts. As I fill out applications now, I cringe. I thank God that I am better, wiser. I wish I had been more like Sylvester. He went to work every day. He would come home, and we would rarely hear him complain. I miss him. I wish I were more like him.

Alone In a Crowd

"Be strong. Be brave. Be fearless. You are never alone."
Joshua 1:9

"I don't want to be alone. I want to be left alone."
Audrey Hepburn

I don't understand it...I can be amongst family or friends and still feel as if I don't belong. I mean, amongst those who genuinely love me, I feel as if I am outside. I have come to the conclusion that it must be the enemy. Because there is no cause for me to feel that way. I can understand it when I am in the midst of those who don't know me or have known me but don't care for me, but this is crazy! I become uncomfortable, then I just get on the phone and begin conducting business or planning an event and I am good again. I have this feeling of detachment and I am safer when I am being productive. I am in the safe place inside myself and no one is allowed in unless I open up to them. I wonder if it's a defense mechanism that I created to protect myself?

Unity

"I in them and you in me—so that they may be brought to complete unity. Then the world will know that you sent me and have loved them even as you have loved me."

John 17:23

"Unity is strength... when there is teamwork and collaboration, wonderful things can be achieved."
— Mattie Stepanek

I sometimes get frustrated in the midst of a worship service. I look out amongst those that claim to know and love Him. Their faces reflect boredom and apathy. It is true that we have trials and afflictions that we endure, but we are living sacrifices. And I genuinely can understand some days where you are just not feeling it, where it seems like you can barely make it through the day. But not every day! Not every Sunday! We operate from a place of victory! We are seated in heavenly places! We need to be teaching people from the moment they get saved about who they are and what they have! Instead, they are witnessing others tell about the hardships they are facing and, to be honest, it sounds as if the devil is the winner! I am so tired of hearing this mess in the Church! We need to submerge ourselves in the Word, not just the reading, either, but listening to true men and women of God during the week as well, who rightly divide the Word of Truth! It is time for us to take our rightful place in the earth, and not seem as if we are the weak ones! No sir! No ma'am! We are more than conquerors! We have already won! In the midst of it all, we have the victory! Remember that! Once we become unified, the miracles, signs and wonders we seek will begin to manifest! It is past time!

50

Second Class Citizen

"But when the fullness of the time had come, God sent forth His Son, born of a woman, born under the law, to redeem those who were under the law, that we might receive the adoption as sons."
Galatians 4:4-5

"The days of humiliation, of second-class citizens and of inequality are over and gone forever."
Gerry Adams

I hate how when you are down and out and need the very people that you made sure were good when you were up and treat you like a second-class citizen. You find out who is truly there for you when you really hit rock bottom...and it is not a good feeling to find out that those who you thought would be rocking with you until the end of time will not find any time for you once you are so far down that it takes God to hold you up or you will snap! It hurt so badly--that is still taking me time to heal from. People would warn me about others, and you know that they aren't lying or misleading you but I still give others the benefit of the doubt. I won't drop one because another says so. But I feel as though nothing I'm saying is being considered or taken seriously since I am not in the position I was before. I had income and I was able to get myself wherever I needed to go. Now I'm unemployed and my license is suspended, so I am dependent upon others to get what I need or get me where I need to go, and it is extremely depressing. I can tell when someone doesn't care to come pick me up to take me where I am going. Or they may come and get me if they are going to the same place--see that I said that THEY MAY! I will never understand human nature. I just thank God that I am born again and have His nature and the Spirit is empowering me to love the whole entire world. That is what keeps me from racking up charges and ending up in jail repeatedly. I still have to talk to myself when it comes to dealing with people, both saved and unsaved. That is what angers me more than anything, probably because I care about people. I don't like dealing with them, but my heart is for them. In spite of it all, I feel for them. I literally feel their pains and heartaches. I bear their burdens sometimes and they don't even know it. And it frustrates me to be treated so unfairly. But I must focus on the One Who saved me, or I will lose my mind...and my salvation! I pray for those who I see going through--these are trying times. We need to be encouraging one another. This should not even have to be said.

The Secret

"The secret of LORD is with those who fear Him, and He will show them His covenant"

Psalm 25:14

"There's a time in your life where you're not quite sure where you are. You think everything's perfect, but it's not perfect... Then one day you wake up and you can't quite picture yourself in the situation you're in. But the secret is, if you can picture yourself doing anything in life, you can do it."

Tom DeLonge

I remember reading a book called "The Secret." It spoke of drawing those things to you that you wish to have by using the power of your mind. Think it and you will have it. It is only reiterating what the Bible says, about renewing your mind and changing your atmosphere, calling those things that be not as though they were. I believe that I call forth the wrong things...I recollect having the use of other people's vehicles. I would be afraid that I would do something to cause it to break down, and it would do so. I was afraid that I would be mistreated in relationships, and it would happen. I was already messed up mentally after believing that my own mother didn't care for me, didn't love me. It was easy to think that no one else would; something must be wrong with me. So, I didn't think that I had good luck. I felt cursed. The first time I broke a mirror, I cried so hard. The person that was with me was so puzzled; all I could see was seven more years of bad luck added to the miserable years I was presently experiencing. The heaviness I carried in my soul I can still recall now, reminiscing on those dark years. Yet, even in these adult years, I battle the darkness trying to overcome me each day. Depression is the leader of the pack and I am victorious in the battle, but it isn't always easy. There are days I would enjoy just remaining in bed and staying under the covers, doing nothing, speaking to no one. I get tired. But there is no one there who would cover me while I was out of order...I have had to have me, have my back. In the end, when I couldn't have my back, it was a war just trying to get people to do the simple things. I felt like discarded trash; I felt as if I were nothing. I had to encourage myself and let me know that in the midst of the storm, I was to fight the good fight of faith. And it was not easy. I am still a warrior. I am proud of myself. Thank God for me. Thank God for His not ever giving up on me.

Prophecy

"I will raise up a prophet like you."
Deuteronomy 18:18

"Maybe I'm the prophet of hip hop for real. Maybe I do come with some kind of divine principle behind me, because I know that every battle I've ever had I've always won."
KRS-One

I know that I am called to be a prophet. I thought that I was nervous about being called to evangelize! No, this is even more agonizing to me! I had been told that I was to be walking in it already, but I had chosen not to--which was absolutely correct. I did not know if I was ready to see some of the things that Stephano was seeing. God had begun to show me things in the Spirit, and I balked! I panicked! And you know, He is a gentleman, so He backed off and waited. So recently, I said that I was all in. Now, mind you, I had forgotten about the prophetic aspect. So, He reminded me. I panicked again but didn't fall back. My pastor began to prophesy over me regarding the prophetic, and he had no clue of what had been transpiring in me! Then a close friend confirmed. And another woman prophesied the same, and she had never met me before that day! So, there is no more excusing and procrastinating. I am now in a prophetic activation class that is showing step by step what to expect, how God operates, dos and don'ts, etc. I did not think that I was qualified to do this. I kept making excuses as to why He should choose someone else. But I am going forth in the Name of Jesus. I will be obedient and speak what He says to me. I will open myself up to the Holy Spirit and know Him even better. I am grateful for Jesus Christ and the things He is doing in my life!

Prayer

"And pray in the Spirit on all occasions with all kinds of prayers and requests. With this in mind, be alert and always keep on praying for all the Lord's people."

Ephesians 6:18

"Prayer is not asking. It is a longing of the soul. It is daily admission of one's weakness. It is better in prayer to have a heart without words than words without a heart."

Mahatma Gandhi

I am so grateful to be in a ministry of prayer. I am a part of Arise Ministries and I found that I am challenged to be better in this area. The founder began a 15-day prayer after being led by the Lord, and my initial thought was, "No way!!" It was to be from 5:50-6:00 AM! We know that I do not do mornings!! But then I felt impressed to set my alarm, so I did. I did not believe that I would be able to stick with this prayer for 15 days. But I found myself awakening and listening in. My day was so much better after doing so. I sat and listened as she prayed for 10 straight minutes and how it changed from day to day, never the same prayer. And in noticing that, I realized that when I pray, I usually pray a routine prayer. It isn't always the same, mind you, but it is the same content. And I made up in my mind to go deeper. I need to know the Holy Spirit more--I feel as though I am only tapping the surface. I made the decision to study even more to get all the meat off the Bible bone and truly be a spiritual scholar. I thank God for having people in my life who inspire without even knowing it. After His removing some of the other people, I really needed those whom He anointed for service. I don't need to be like them, but I can be the best I can be for His glory.

Family

"But as for me and my household, we will serve the LORD."
Joshua 24:15

"The bond that links your true family is not one of blood, but of respect and joy in each other's life."
Richard Bach

I am not one who goes to family gatherings much. Or go to anything like that for that matter. I am a homebody, preferring to Netflix and chill. I am called to evangelize and put on events for His glory, and I am obedient in that, but people think that I am all outgoing and am a people person, but it isn't like that. I do love people, but am not a people person, if that makes sense. I want my family to know that I love them, but I am not one to be in your face and your business all the time. My son and I even separate in order to regroup following an event. I just have to get alone to build myself back up. It seems to take a lot out of me when I am out ministering--and I consider my life to be ministry, because I have found out you never know when someone will need you, and you are praying or encouraging or edifying. People are hurting, and I know the solution. I believe my family knows I love them, even though I do not make it to the parties or the cookouts. They know my schedule. I see their accomplishments on social media, or I may hear it from friends or other family members. I am proud

of my family. I love them dearly. And this chapter is a shout out
to you all. Keep pressing and continue to be great!

Marital Problems

"Husbands, love your wives, as Christ loved the church and gave himself up for her, that he might sanctify her, having cleansed her by the washing of water with the word, so that he might present the church to himself in splendor, without spot or wrinkle or any such thing, that she might be holy and without blemish. In the same way husbands should love their wives as their own bodies. He who loves his wife loves himself. For no one ever hated his own flesh, but nourishes and cherishes it, just as Christ does the church..."
Ephesians 5:25-33

"When people get married because they think it's a long-time love affair, they'll be divorced very soon, because all love affairs end in disappointment. But marriage is a recognition of a spiritual identity."
Joseph Campbell

I never would have thought that people would take the time to destroy a person's marriage, or any relationship for that matter. But seeing what I have seen thus far, it is happening far too often. I got married and was told point blank that people didn't like the fact that we were together and would attempt to sabotage it. I didn't believe that, because who takes out quality time from their lives to destroy someone else's relationship without cause? Just because they feel like it? I was amazed at how messy things became after the marriage and how much I believed what was said. Not that all were lies, but just the fact that I was drawn into the messiness and became some entirely different person who was unhappy and lost trust in others. I am sure that I was an amusement to many during that time. At one point, I stopped speaking to everyone, because I didn't even know who I could trust. Now I am wary of anyone-- after being burned by people who set up laughing in my face, being deceitful behind my back. I think it sad that you cannot deal with those who are made in His image, even those that profess His Name. It was one sister, my sister by another mother, who was straight up with me from the jump about what was going on behind my back. And I heard that she was setting idiots straight even when I wasn't present. That is a rarity--and I will never forget it. That was one of the worst times in my life, but it was a time when I learned some of my most important lessons. At that time, I was someone who I had said I would never be. I was angry and disappointed and said things I should not have said, done things I said I would never do. You really see how you will react and respond once you are really in the midst of a situation. You just never know... I grew up during a time when locked doors weren't necessary. When people would rally together to help one another. When family was important, and children were protected. Things are changing, and not for the better. That is distressing when you have seen the way things were and how it was uplifting the family and encouraging unity. Now there is little respect for what was at one time considered sacred. The enemy is definitely on his job. I wish that we as Christians were just as determined.

Time

"Making the best use of the time, because the days are evil."
Ephesians 5:16

"Learn to enjoy every minute of your life. Be happy now. Don't wait for something outside of yourself to make you happy in the future. Think how really precious the time is you have to spend, whether it's at work or with your family. Every minute should be enjoyed and savored."
Earl Nightingale

I consider my time a very valuable commodity. I have usually outlined my days, weeks, shoot--even months! I think it rude when I tell someone ahead of time, "I have this amount of time to spend with you, talk to you, counsel you" or whatever the case may be, but the individual will take up that time and then some, with no regards for my next appointment. I am trying not to get to the point where I walk off or hang up, because I feel that is extremely rude, but I am going to have to do something to let people know that I am serious about my time. A lot of the questions, concerns or scenarios that these people put out for me to deal with can be taken care of if they were in the Word faithfully, attending a good Bible Study, or sitting in an event that I am hosting. Much of what they come to me for has been dealt with and there are testimonies, amazing testimonies that they have missed out on while they sit at home while I am doing the work of the Kingdom. Now don't get me wrong--I don't mind assisting and helping those that need it, because that is what I am here for. But coming to me for the same thing and refusing to do what I instruct you biblically, then you are determined to stay where you are. And that is cool. But just be real with me on it, so I can schedule you a block of time for you to release, then we move on to the next. But I am not one to sit and listen to you whine about something you are not going to do anything about. It is draining. Especially while I am dealing with my own issues and trying to maintain the line, and I am still there for others as well, who will not extend the same courtesy to me. I just pray that God continues to grace me and give me discernment on who to continue with and who to bless with counsel, prayers, then a godly release. I see how people see me tired, drained, worn out but still pull on me with selfish reasons. That will no longer be acceptable. It is getting to where they are demanding my time, as if I have clocked in and they are paying me. No more. I am done.

Church

"And I tell you, you are Peter, and on this rock I will build my church, and the gates of hell shall not prevail against it."
Matthew 16:18

"We come to church not to hide our problems but to heal them."
Dieter F. Uchtdorf

I am crazy enough to believe that this world can operate as the apostles and disciples did in the Book of Acts. There can be miracles, signs and wonders evident in the earth! In most ministries, there are people gathering, but for what reason? Tradition? Habit? Curiosity? I see the faces of the congregation at the various ministries, and I am concerned. It looks as though the majority doesn't even want to be present. There is no lifting of hands, no singing, no praising--and I understand that everyone doesn't worship in the same way, but there should be some sign of life! It saddens me to glance over the people and see the apathy or the boredom. I truly don't believe that they understand what would happen if we would get on one accord! The things that would happen in the midst of a people that were of one mind and coming together in unity! There would be no need for anyone to request that hands be laid upon them or a prayer line--for the Lord of Hosts would Himself enter in and the Spirit of God would touch the entire Church Body and there will be testimonies that would astound and inspire the world! We don't care anymore. We come to worship service and don't even turn down our phones so that it doesn't disturb the pastor. We allow our children to be on the tablets and we aren't teaching them the word of God in our home. We are a complacent lot, who are more concerned about satisfying ourselves than seeking God. It is depressing and it hurts me to see. I can only imagine how He feels. Lord, help us to see You and be like You in this earth. We are failing miserably. The world is looking to drugs, sex, and other religions, including satanism, to fill the void that is within. We have the solution, but we are holding onto it like it's a secret that we are to guard, instead of the Gospel we are to spread.

Creativity

"Do you see a man skillful in his work? He will stand before kings; he will not stand before obscure men."
Proverbs 22:29

"The comfort zone is the great enemy to creativity; moving beyond it necessitates intuition, which in turn configures new perspectives and conquers fears."
Dan Stevens

I thank God for the gifts that He has placed in me. I am amazed at the visions that He gives me and how He extraordinarily brings them to pass in such a way that blesses and encourages His people. So many will approach me after an event and tell me that it was exactly what they needed and how it should continue. It tickles me because I was only doing what was instructed, often asking, "What the world"?????? It was something so out of the ordinary that I just knew I would look crazy...well, crazier!! But the work of the Lord is awesome! It is uncomfortable sometimes, stepping out of that comfort zone into purpose and destiny, especially when you look at you and see nothing close to what He is asking you to do. But I look at Him with eyes full of faith and trust, and I strut out on His Word and watch Him accomplish what He will! He is glorious and I thank God He shines upon me! I will press forward in my calling with gratitude since He thought enough of me to use me to bring Heaven to Earth! I used to think that I was worthless...now I laugh at that notion! I am honored to be in a relationship with the One Who Created the universe and then made man in His image and likeness. And the fact that I have the same Spirit in me that raised Jesus Christ from the dead is BOSS!!! You can't tell me nothing!! (Very bad grammar, but I want it just like that!! I know you can hear me say that just like that, for those who know me well!)

I am looking forward to what He is planning to do through me, and I am awaiting the glory in the midst of the people as He does it! There is no one like Him, and there is no one like me!! I said what I said! I'm crushing on myself!! I love her! I didn't always, but now...what a beauty she is!! What a peculiar princess! What a jewel in His diadem!! Yeah, that Stephanie!

Dismissal

"For they deliberately overlook this fact, that the heavens existed long ago, and the earth was formed out of water and through water by the word of God,"

2 Peter 3:5

"I was not depressed when they got me out. I have always taken my dismissals as part of the game."

Frank Woolley

It's sad. I have noticed how many people will disregard the words that I say. Even those who will reach out to me for a consultation or counseling will dismiss the counsel given, and they will still do as they please. Why did you even ask me for anything? That was a waste of both our time and energy to even meet! Nothing has changed at all. I notice how I will say something, and I know for a fact that it is beneficial or necessary. Then the individual ignores it, but later down the line issues come up due to the fact he/she didn't follow the suggestions, then they return to me to help them fix the problem! I just wanted to call them "Stupid!!!" In the beginning, I would be crazy enough to straighten out the problems, but then I realized that I was as stupid as they were! If I give you the answer and you refuse to do it, then don't come to me when everything blows up in your face! Me, with my idiotic self, helping them and wasting good valuable time when they didn't consider my words valuable enough to consider.

I don't understand sometimes. I need to begin asking questions like, "Are you looking for answers or you just want to vent?" Because some people are looking to be heard and not to be healed. That will save us both time and energy. Cause I can just sit and listen and not have to say or do anything. Then we can carry on with no expectations and no disappointments. Simple and easy! My kind of transaction.

I experience dismissal even in ministry. I will be preaching/teaching and the looks on the faces of the congregation can be disheartening. I see why in the Old Testament, it says, "Be not afraid of their faces!" These folks can look crazy sometimes! But I know that I am called, and nothing shall deter me, so they can continue to look crazy and I will continue to do what I was created to do. It is discouraging, and everyone cannot deal with the way that people will do you as you walk this journey on the earth. But I will remain focused on what I am to do while I walk here.

Anxiety

"Casting all your anxieties on him, because he cares for you."
1 Peter 5:7

"I never thought I'd be somebody dealing with anxiety or
depression."
Ileana D'Cruz

I am 48-years-old and still have to overcome anxiety when I
am in different places or around certain people. There are times
when I am feeling not so complete and so unworthy and I have to
talk to myself in that firm, not taking no mess tone and tell myself
that I belong wherever it is and I am worthy to do whatever it is
that I am present to do! Who is going to stop me? Nobody, not
even me! Outsiders looking in swear that I have it all together and
nothing is ever tormenting me--or trying to. The devil is a whole
lie! I am walking in my purpose and the enemy is fixated on
stopping this movement, but what I won't do is allow him or
broadcast it! Most of the time I suffer in silence or only speak with
a few. I have been there when I shared with people, I just knew
that I could trust...and my business was out there for others to
know. It hurt me, but wounds heal, and I learn to do better.
Everyone isn't your friend, and that may include some of the ones

that we think are our friends. Then people wonder why you have fallen back and slacked up on the communication. Baby, it's because you did too much in your communication and it has hindered our communication! To be betrayed by the very ones you commended and praised to others for their confidentiality is more painful than can be expressed. But I am yet alive! I am still going forward. I am still winning! I am a victor, a conqueror, and I continue to triumph!! In spite of pain, I still gained! So now I need to go forth and be anxious for nothing, for I have overcome some of the very things I thought that I just wouldn't survive.

Death

"For if we live, we live to the Lord, and if we die, we die to the Lord. So then, whether we live or whether we die, we are the Lord's."
Romans 14:8

"The fear of death follows from the fear of life. A man who lives fully is prepared to die at any time."
Mark Twain

I don't usually go to funerals. I attended my aunt's funeral today and it was so bittersweet. The Lord is speaking to me during the funeral and he is comforting my soul with the thought of her stepping out of her earth body and her spirit entering the glory of Heaven! It was rough, because I could feel the pain and sorrow of the family and friends, but the joy of knowing where she is and Who she is with was overwhelming! If only the atmosphere could have been opened and the family could see the present state of their loved one! It is a sight to behold! I can only imagine the reunion of her and her mother and father, of her sisters and brothers!!! My God, the glory!!!! No more suffering and pain, no sorrow, no weariness! I enjoy my time and my people here, but the day that I am separated from this body and take on immortality...I rejoice in knowing that her life spoke volumes--many expressed it today. She touched people wherever she went. I am in prayer for the family. But I pray that they are comforted with the Truth. Death is only transition from here to there. And there is so much better!! We live to live again!!

Community Involvement

"Let the elders who rule well be considered worthy of double
honor, especially those who labor in preaching and teaching."
1 Timothy 5:17

"We have to provide good teachers, a good environment,
community involvement with schools."
David Selby

I am one who is not much for talking when there is something
to be done. I am one who when I see a need, I will fill the need, or
seek out someone qualified to do so. My husband lost a niece to
gun violence, followed by consecutive gun violence deaths after
hers in the span of less than a week. People were all over
Facebook talking about something needs to be done, but these
same people were nowhere to be found in the scheduled meetings
that occurred. So that shows me that you aren't about that life.
You are one to sit and chat about the things going on in the world,
but you are reluctant to get your hands in on the solution. It
bothered me that I couldn't get to all the meetings, but I know that I
can help in some shape or form with the ones that I did get to. I
thank God for those individuals who did step up and have meetings
and those who attended and committed their time and energy to
getting a solution for these misguided youth. It should have been

an ongoing deal, but many times people don't step up until a
tragedy occurs. I am looking for change in the community and it
begins with me. I am willing to put my foot to the pedal to begin
getting answers for our problems. I pray that others join in and
make this a major movement.

Behind the Curtain

"But when you pray, go into your room and shut the door and pray to your Father who is in secret. And your Father who sees in secret will reward you."

Matthew 6:6

"I almost died, secretly, behind closed doors."

Stephen Baldwin

People never really know what goes on behind the scenes of the ones who are truly seeking the Kingdom first...the outward glory that is seen is the evidence of a life that is being crushed inwardly. I thank God for the glory of God that is seen in my life, but whew! The trials and tribulations that occur on a daily basis has me and my weaponry busy winning! I tell you, when I was running from my calling as an evangelist, I thought I was just running from that single responsibility, though I do not take it lightly. It is a huge responsibility to be chosen to go carry the Kingdom mandate to the ones who have not received it yet. But it is more than that. You must be disciplined in every area of life. You must be willing to stand alone and face ridicule or persecution from the ones you just knew for sure would be on your side. You must continue to be strong when family and friends will turn their backs on you for the dumbest of reasons. You must be resilient when you are doing the majority of the work amongst a hundred able bodied but hardheaded people who call themselves ministering as you do, but with no evidence. You must speak when it appears as though no one is listening to you, when you wish to shut up, but the calling is calling and you answer every time in the affirmative. You must stand tall and unyielding when you are misunderstood and rejected by the individuals you assisted with your whole being and they speak against you in your face without guilt or shame, as if you were in the enemy's camp. You must be rooted and grounded to go forth when you are tired in your whole soul! You must be steadfast and immovable when your body is aching, and you do not feel like being anyone's minister! Jesus Christ went through so much for us. I can definitely live for Him with all that I endure behind the ministry title. I want Him to be glorified. And He shall be. Watch!!!

Apathy

"Wake up, and strengthen what remains and is about to die, for I have not found your works complete in the sight of my God."
Revelations 3:2

"We may have found a cure for most evils; but we have found no remedy for the worst of them all, the apathy of human beings."
Helen Keller

I just cannot understand it. I live amongst people who do not care about others. I cannot comprehend it; I am determined to do all I can to spiritually impact those around me. I am going to show those I come in contact with who Jesus is. I reach out to the members of this community and receive turned up noses and attitudes! And my flesh wants to turn mine up in return and let them know that they are nowhere near all that they believe they are! We are in this TOGETHER! We need to open our eyes to what is going on and join hands in getting solutions to these problems! Everyone is concerned about me and mine, while not realizing that in a moment, we could be in a similar situation. I am touched when I read of those who have reached superstar status, who continually contribute their earnings to charities and needy families around the world. If we all did but a little, it would be for the greater good. I see as I plan an event for the homeless how selfish some people—even some ministries—really are. And it's disheartening. It's sad. But I am more angered than anything. And to have to learn to deal with the anger and still exhibit the love of God is taxing and challenging. I refuse to allow anything to defeat me or my purpose in this journey. And I will battle the forces that come against me, whether it be man or spirit. The will of God will be done in my life. And that includes assisting the needy. It should be the work of the Church as a whole, but appears the ministries are more comfortable within the four walls, preaching and teaching a gospel that they aren't fulfilling. That's paradoxical. Mike Murdock said that whatever angers you is something that you are to be the solution to. I have the solution. Anger consumes me in a way that moves me. Watch me burn and bring answers to questions and issues that are being ignored. God and me—majority!!

Mornings

"And God called the expanse Heaven. And there was evening and there was morning, the second day."
Genesis 1:8

"When you arise in the morning, think of what a precious privilege it is to be alive - to breathe, to think, to enjoy, to love."
Marcus Aurelius

I am not a morning person. I enjoy the evenings. I have always worked third shift with no issues, none with remaining awake or with not sleeping. It is my most difficult time of the day, and I have no reason for it at all. It is the fiercest battle for me, is my waking up and starting a good day. The battle immediately begins in my mind even before opening my eyes. It is generally a battle with depression. I could have no reason at all to be depressed, but I deal with it regardless. I awaken and the fight is on! I battle not wanting to get out of bed, feeling like there is no reason to exist, when I know my purpose and callings and are fulfilling them! I feel as though I have the weight of the world on my entire body and I struggle to get up and get moving. I have battled it for as long as I can remember, even in my youth. I was not successful in my younger years in defeating it. I make sure that when it comes now, I address it and let it know that I am the winner, the conqueror, the victor! The enemy will continue to attack with what was successful for him before...but I like to change the odds in my favor! The Name of Jesus is above every other name, including depression, but that doesn't mean that you won't be tested and tried! I just continue to come out on top in spite of! I was so depressed when I was younger that it teamed up with suicide and I was going to take myself out of here! It truly appeared to be the only solution to me. I genuinely believed that the world would be better without me in it, for I felt that I wasn't doing anything anyway. I thank God that I am more than a conqueror and that He causes me to triumph every time!

Numbness

"For the word of God is living and active, sharper than any two-edged sword, piercing to the division of soul and of spirit, of joints and of marrow, and discerning the thoughts and intentions of the heart."

Hebrews 4:12

When you're in survival mode, you numb yourself.
Clemantine Wamariya

I just want to say this...I think of how the body goes into shock when it has sustained great injury or harm...and I have been feeling this way for a couple of weeks after being misunderstood and mistreated. It has been years since someone has done it to me, after getting to know me personally and spending time with me, then turning and accusing me of something I would never do and then sharing with others who don't have a clue, but who support them in their crusade of lies. I am one who will be there with you until the wheels fall off, and if you look beside you and I come up missing, then you need to check yourself for something you did. For I am the individual who will give you multiple chances when you have messed up, for I feel sympathetic to your plight. I give way too many chances for someone to hurt me, allowing them in my space when they should have been cut off years ago. And that's my fault. I enabled it. I admit it. Thinking people will rise up and be who they are called to be, being better than what they are presently. I can be with you and see past the mess you are, the mess you bring, to show you the love of Jesus and aid you in whatever you need. But when one perceives that I have done something, imagined usually, there is a full-fledged rally going on! Not common sense kicking in and saying, "Look, idiot, this chick has been in it with you for a minute now, so let's rethink this! Let us go talk to her if we feel this way so we can get this straightened out." I have had a lineup of people coming at me sideways and talking slick. Thank God for maturity. I could have acted a whole 'nother way and it wouldn't have been cute. But God. I thank God that I am in Him. I still have to let it go and forgive these folk...I can feel heat up in my chest when I think of it, so I know it's time to release that issue. I am going to walk in the Spirit and get all that God has for me. I will see signs, miracles, and wonders. I will stand before Him and hear Him say, "Well done." I am not concerned about these folks and what they have going on, but I am going to pray for everyone trippin' because they need it. And I am going to double prayer for me, because if this continues, then I am going to need it! I have been to jail twice, and that is enough!! But seriously, I am becoming numb to certain things, and I don't like it. I know it is a defense mechanism, but I don't want to be sitting around feeling nothing at all. Even the hurt is better, for I am feeling something. I am dealing with my own inner surgery while on the spiritual table. It is painful for me, but it will be done. I will be totally healed. I decree and declare that to myself and it is so!! I ain't playing with me or anyone else when it comes to ministry.

Obedience

"Why do you call me 'Lord, Lord,' and not do what I tell you?"
Luke 6:46

"Obedience opens the door to the constant companionship of the Holy Ghost. And the spiritual gifts and abilities activated by the power of the Holy Ghost enable us to avoid deception - and to see, to feel, to know, to understand, and to remember things as they really are."

David A. Bednar

I know that God is pleased with me. I know that many are like, "What????!! How can she say that??" But I am serious. I thank God that God is pleased with me. I am one of the obedient children. I am concerned about my walk with Him. I will assist others, of course, I am my brother's keeper. But I concentrate on being willing and obedient to the One Who created me. I want to commune with Him each day and draw closer and closer to Him. I want to do the things that He has for me to do. I feel Him walking with me throughout the day, and I cannot express what that means to me. I remember living life and hating it. I was miserable and was going through life trying to make others around me just as miserable, too. I couldn't stand to see anyone happy! I am so serious! Now to have the Spirit of Christ be with me 24/7 is such a blessing! I feel honored and privileged! I wake up and sometimes that depression is about to jump me, but the Lord is there, and He is mightier than any other name or disease or trial I face! It is like having that one child who is always trying to please you. I want to be her! I am not saying that others aren't. I'm saying, their walk is not my concern. I am happy for them. They are my family. But this thing is personal to me! I have to do what I am called to do. I already took too long in carrying out His wishes! I just knew that I was too unworthy to do anything for Him. The Word determined that was a lie! I am proud to be a daughter of the King! I will bring glory to His Name for as long as I live!

Expectation

"Beloved, we are God's children now, and what we will be has not yet appeared; but we know that when he appears we shall be like him, because we shall see him as he is."

1 John 3:2

"For me, a life without expectation results in a life with inspiration."

Alanis Morissette

I was speaking with a sister last night and she said something true but disappointing. She said, "Don't expect anything out of anyone and you won't be disappointed." And I see the truth in this, but where it is disappointing is here: if I have expectations of a ministry and they don't come through with what they are supposed to be and do, then what good are they? I feel like I should have expectations of a ministry, or family, or friends, not expecting them to be there all the time or fulfilling my every need, but if you cannot do the very things your name requires, then what good are you to me or to anyone else? The Church is to teach and preach the Kingdom and save, heal, deliver, etc. and if they are not, then they are useless. Family is a support system that should have your back and if they are never there, then they are not the true definition of family. I'm expecting a grocery store to have food, a gas station to have gas, and a beauty supply store to have beauty supplies. So, it isn't unreasonable for me to expect something from someone. It angers me that the world can talk about the Church and it is nothing but the truth! In the Bible, the Church was taking care of business and turning the world upside down! They were feared and were in the Kingdom business of casting out demons, healing the sick, raising the dead and overcoming the power of the enemy! Now I have sat through services and felt as though I wasted three whole hours of my whole life in the midst of mess! This is unacceptable! Plain and simple, I can depend upon those who I do not know intimately before the ones I can who I support regularly! And I am not talking about those who are fulfilling their purpose, for they are as busy as I am. People know what they are doing and who they will do it for. And let it be so but let me be as well. If you don't wish to support my vision, then be blind to my calling as well, unless God Himself has you to reach out and contact me. And that has happened. And when I went to refuse, the Spirit spoke to me and told me to accept the invitation, when I really didn't want to. And afterwards, I was made to see why. So, my expectations are still there, but I realize that everyone is not being who or what they should be, so I can and will experience disappointments. But I pray that we rise up to be all that we should be and live a higher standard than what we have been, for this is truly sorry!

Uselessness

"And seeing a fig tree by the wayside, he went to it and found nothing on it but only leaves. And he said to it, "May no fruit ever come from you again!" And the fig tree withered at once."
Matthew 21:19

"Everyone loves feeling comfortable. But it's actually completely useless."

Tobias Lutke

I have noticed that I can be in the midst of a worship service, or any event or workshop that is supposed to be focusing or promoting God but will be utterly bored. And I check myself first, because I ask myself if I am disconnected and need to release something--am I blocking my own blessing? But even while looking around to gauge the reactions of others, the entire atmosphere is of complacency and/or indifference. I come seeking the atmosphere that will set captives free and heal the wounded, but when you attempt to get into His presence, you can feel the weight, the spirit of heaviness in the room. I have experienced the atmosphere where the Church began to praise and worship in unity and the Spirit of the Lord was manifested and miracles were present! I remember vividly being in the midst of a worship service where the people came expecting and lifted their hands and voices to God and He came and did signs, miracles, and wonders!!! Sometimes I feel as though the entire church service was useless. I could have done more sitting in my room reading or praying or writing. I was actually angry that I had come expecting and had left empty. Then I had to go talk to myself and ask if I had sincerely approached with praise and worship if I was so easily distracted by the things going on around me. And I found it to be that I was focused on the atmosphere and the people more than on my Father when my circumstances were not so favorable. When I was in need of a touch from the Master and I was needing some encouragement from my brothers and sisters. Usually I am the one who is uplifting and edifying and trying to let the people know that whatever they are going through will pass and to keep their heads up and press forward! But others will see you as strong and won't reach out to return the favor, thinking that you have it all together, not realizing that you are in need of prayer and encouragement just like they do! How hard is that to comprehend? In my anger, I have called people useless! They are sitting there doing nothing but wanting everything! They are desiring the most and doing the least. I just pray more and thank my Creator for being One Who is sustaining me!

Voices

"There are, it may be, so many kinds of voices in the world, and none of them is without signification."
1 Corinthians 14:10

"This stand wasn't because I feel like I'm being put down in any kind of way. This is because I'm seeing things happen to people that don't have a voice: people that don't have a platform to talk and have their voices heard and affect change. So, I'm in the position where I can do that, and I'm going to do that for people that can't."
Colin Kaepernick

When you walk in your life there will be many voices speaking to you, including your speaking to yourself. There are many good meaning people, but that doesn't mean that they have your best interests at heart. They may desire the best for you, but that doesn't mean they know the path that God has for you. I have had plenty of people chiming in on my life and what I should do, not knowing what was going on in my life, nor were they assisting me in any way to do better or be better! Thank God for the few who spoke and took action, helping me to progress and mature in the things that God had for me, for it propelled me to my destiny and I still continue on today! It can be confusing trying to discern who to listen to, for everyone is not meaning you harm, but God's voice is paramount, and we line up with what He says and we walk out His will. The walk will be a distinct one, for the one who walks with God stands out from among the rest. They are truly a set apart people. They speak differently. They live differently. They respond differently. As God's people, Israel was recognized as His people. They were revered and feared because the people knew that God was on their side. Are we seen as the people of God? Are we noticed because of the anointing? Does He reside in us and radiate through us? In the beginning, my own negative voice drowned out any other voices, including those who truly loved me. I could not hear or receive that. I was worthless and unlovable and angry. I didn't need any haters because I was my number one enemy. I told myself things that I should never have said. I treated her awfully and I have had to apologize to her. My own voice should have been hope to myself. I thank God that He came and saved me. I am eternally grateful. Now I am particular about who I listen to. The Word must go forth and it must be for me!!

Miscommunication

"Avoid miscommunication. The price you pay for it is horrendous."

Shiv Sherka

I can tell you right now, that I am obviously NOT a good communicator. I used to believe that I was. I am a poet and can place words so beautifully and skillfully that I even impact myself! But in speaking with others and seeing that what I have said twisted around terribly, I am seeking to be clearer when it comes to the things I make vocal! I know that sometimes people will genuinely know what you're talking about but will choose to misunderstand or not understand at all--you can see them for what they are. The questions that are asked with skepticism, the smirks on the face, and the knowing looks that scream out that you're an idiot, when you are totally aware that what you're saying makes complete sense. I don't understand the issues that people have, to keep division alive instead of trying to see things from another perspective, taking a walk in someone else's shoes. I am the one who will listen to someone for hours, hearing the pain and feeling the burden of anguish, and I feel for them, and I thank God for being there to listen to them and allow them to free themselves and just be unburdened. That means a lot---and a lot of individuals are not receiving it. They are carrying their heavy loads with them everywhere they go, and it is taking a toll on their lives. I sit in disappointment as I pass ministry after ministry on the street, but I see those ministry's members and they are weighed down with troubles. I can relate, as I am often misunderstood as I am speaking, and it is made to seem as though I am saying something completely different from what was intended. If they would just listen to what I am saying, and even what I am not saying, as one author stated, then we would communicate so much better. I pray that I become more and more adept in listening and communicating so there is no equivocation when it comes to understanding the message that I am conveying. I pray that I am one who listens without speaking before they finish so that I can be the one who fully gets their meaning. Help me to be more like You, Lord. Thank You for clarity when it comes to the things I need to see and hear and speak.

Naysayers

"And you will be dragged before governors and kings for my sake, to bear witness before them and the Gentiles. When they deliver you over, do not be anxious how you are to speak or what you are to say, for what you are to say will be given to you in that hour. For it is not you who speak, but the Spirit of your Father speaking through you."

Matthew 10:18-20

"If you want to do something different, you're going to come up against a lot of naysayers."

James Dyson

I wish that I could honestly say that those who do say that it won't come to pass or that I am not hearing from God really didn't affect me. Now I am definitely not talking about those who don't know me at all--you have very little regard when it comes to me and I don't value your opinion. I am talking about those who are close to me and come to me saying "Yea, hath God said?" like that sneaky serpent in the Garden. He said that My sheep know my voice, and I know I do. If you do not agree, take that thing up with the Lord and keep it moving. I have done enough second guessing to last me a whole lifetime. I was a professional at it until about a year ago when I got an attitude with myself and told her that she is good enough to receive the blessings of God! I was so mean to her and always spoke down to her, but she is free from the curse and has an inheritance! She will eat the good of the land! I will no longer be a part of the crew that will doubt what God can do in my life. I have to lift myself up from the abyss after listening to family and friends (so-called?) tell me that what God said was negative or not true. I have never had to stand as firm as I have these past 2 years when I became completely sold out to God. I cannot live my life based on what He has told you to do with yours. We are on the same path but with different maps. We are headed to Heaven but getting there in different ways. I have never been more sure of what He is doing in my life, probably because I have never been paying more attention! I love where I am and where God is taking me. This is where I have longed to be for years. I am honored to be considered for the positions that He has me fulfilling. God Himself knows I would not have asked for them. I am excited to see what He will do through me for His glory. I am expecting to see signs, miracles and wonders following His Word in this season and for the rest of my life!

Imperfection

"For all have sinned and fall short of the glory of God,"
Romans 3:23

"I think every single imperfection adds to your beauty. I'd rather be imperfect than perfect."

Sonam Kapoor

I went on Facebook Live earlier and spoke on how tired I was of hearing people say, "I'm not perfect," or "I'm only human." Jesus spoke in Matthew 5:48 and said, "Be ye perfect as I am perfect." If He says we can be perfect, then it is so. People are looking at their imperfections and shortcomings when we should be looking to Jesus, who is the Author and Finisher of our faith and can do above and beyond all that we can ever ask or think. But here we are focusing on what we cannot do, when He has given us everything pertaining to life and godliness. We are empowered from within and we can accomplish for Him and because of Him far more than we could ever imagine! He has placed us here for a purpose and we are to fulfill it. He is not looking at us as imperfect or flawed for we have been covered by the Blood and we are the righteousness of God in Christ! We are His sons and daughters, and He desires a relationship with us! He longs to speak with us daily. But all you can focus on is what's wrong with you? Please! We need to soak in the Word and apply it after reading and studying so we can walk worthy of the calling. We have our own paths, and we are to reach select people, but we are concentrating on what we are unable to do! Stop it! Our perception of our flawed selves stops nothing else--we still get jobs, have children, start businesses, with all the things wrong with us, but when it comes to ministry, we have a million excuses! I know this, for I was once there! But we are in the time now where it is no time for this nonsense! The end times are the times we are walking in and we know it for sure! And we are failing to reach the ones we are assigned to because we are in a corner crying over what we see wrong with us. It is time for us to stand up--and take a stand! I see handicapped individuals who lack arms or legs who are living full and productive lives, but the ones who have everybody part working effectively are not using their bodies for the work of the Lord! That's sad! That is dysfunctional! And this is where we are. We do more crying and whining than moving and shaking. And we are too powerful a people to do this! We need to stop talking defeat and begin speaking victoriously!

Disconnect

"Do not be conformed to this world, but be transformed by the
renewal of your mind, that by testing you may discern what is the
will of God, what is good and acceptable and perfect."
Romans 12:2

"The more in harmony with yourself you are, the more joyful you
are and the more faithful you are. Faith is not to disconnect you
from reality - it connects you to reality."
Paulo Coelho

There are days here recently where I feel disconnected from the
presence of God. I know that the teacher is silent during the test. I
hate the emptiness that seems to come in when you do not sense
that comforting presence of the Almighty One, the One Who never
leaves nor forsakes. In this present battle, I awaken to begin
addressing the Holy Spirit while not even "feeling" the presence.
That is definitely why we must walk by faith and not by sight. If
we try to live by what we perceive with these natural senses, we
will fail. Even in the natural realm, I get mixed signals from those
around me--or I am the one mixing them up myself! So, I must
depend on the Word and continue to follow the precepts, even

when the storms hinder my vision. I will be in a service, but it seems like the Spirit isn't touching a part of my soul and I am not whole or impacted by the glory manifesting in the building. I know Who He is and what He does, but it is as if I am standing on the outside looking in. I am praying and decreeing and seeing things happen for others as it appears that nothing has moved in my own life. I have to trust Him in the midst of this. I have come too far and will not get off course. One misstep can get you so far from your destination. I will not fail.

Biblical Foundation

"Therefore thus says the Lord God, "Behold, I am the one who has laid as a foundation in Zion, a stone, a tested stone, a precious cornerstone, of a sure foundation: 'Whoever believes will not be in haste.'"

Isaiah 28:16

"We can never learn too much of His will towards us, too much of His messages and His advice. The Bible is His word, and its study gives at once the foundation for our faith and an inspiration to battle onward in the fight against the tempter."

John D. Rockefeller

I thank God for the leaders who taught me genuine foundational and practical truths. I was often dismissed by those who I looked to for guidance and it was crushing. I was already dealing with it from childhood and just thought of it as the continuing issue that I was just going to have to deal with. Who would have thought that those over you would be intimidated by you, or would try to hold you back out of spite or insecurity? I thank God that as I walked with Him, He began to place those in my path who were willing to be spiritual father/mother to me and show me that a spiritual family is real. I want to be one who pushes anyone I am responsible for into their purpose. Why would anyone want to hold their child back from their destiny? You are jealous of your own child? The things that I have seen have thrown me for a loop sometimes. Many times, a spiritual family is just as bad as a bad physical family! I am growing in the knowledge of the Lord Jesus Christ and I am so glad about it. I am learning how to deal with others when it comes to how they are acting--there is no need for me to react or respond the majority of the time, because it isn't about me. They have their own issues, and they must deal with those on their own. It is very hurtful, but it isn't something to stop me at all, as it would have before. I used to think that something was wrong with me, because these things kept happening to me. Now I recognize the enemy for who he is, and I know that I am walking in my purpose, allowing God to have His way in my life, and I am undeterred by man!

Heartbreak

"The Lord is near to the brokenhearted and saves the crushed in spirit. Many are the afflictions of the righteous, but
the Lord delivers him out of them all. He keeps all his bones; not one of them is broken."

Psalm 34:18-20

"There is no better than adversity. Every defeat, every heartbreak, every loss, contains its own seed, its own lesson on how to improve your performance the next time."

Malcolm X

I have recently been separated from two individuals whom I thought were placed in my life for life. I knew God had sent them to me--it was confirmed to me and I felt it, even if confirmation had not occurred. But it wasn't long after that they both stopped speaking or communicating with me--both at the very same time. I feel as though it is something to that, but I cannot prove anything. Now I know that people are placed into our lives for a season only and we know seasons do not last long. I just wish that the joy that I had with these individuals would have lasted longer. But I do not wish to have anyone there whom the Lord God does not plan for me to have. And as much as it hurts me right now and how I sometimes burst into tears at the loss, I will press on and continue to do as I am called to do. I miss them and still love them and want God's very best for them. I hate sometimes being out of control-- enduring things that I cannot control. Yet, I am fully aware that I serve the One Who is always in control of my life and I trust Him. My circle has never been large, so this isn't some devastating event in my life. But these are two who brought great joy to my life and I wouldn't have chosen to have them absent. Life goes on. You heal. And I will. I had begun to question myself, asking what I had done wrong and how I offended...when I realized I was regressing into old habits where I was always the one at fault, no matter what anyone did--I blamed myself and excused the other party. I immediately stopped myself and released any feelings of guilt, blame, and shame. I refused to accept anything other than what I truly was. That weight of negativity would have brought me down greatly, and at this time, I do not need that! It would result in my domino effect downfall. I am going to persevere and be made whole as God originally intended.

Mouthy

"Set a guard, O Lord, over my mouth; keep watch over the door of my lips!"

Psalm 141:3

"Since everyone has a mouth, everyone will have an opinion."
Ram Gopal Varma

I am flabbergasted by the number of Christians who state, "I am going to let them know what I think--they aren't running over me!" But these same people will not make a sound when asked to pray out loud. They will look surprised and say that they cannot do it. First of all, how is that even possible? You are running off at the mouth, getting loud and being obnoxious, looking stupid in front of people who generally don't even care about what you think or feel or not, bringing reproach to the Name of the One you swear to love so much, but when asked to speak to Him, you refuse. I am confused. You are obviously not prioritizing your life to begin with, but if you can loudly berate someone for whatever reason, then you can most certainly use that mouth to give glory where it truly belongs--to God! We are not called to be doormats, and I understand that completely, but you also aren't called to be silent where prayer is concerned. Our prayers give the One Who created us permission to come in our situations and have His way. He is the God of the earth, but He gave us dominion on the earth, and we must invite Him here to do what He needs to do. We are quicker to tell someone off viciously than to give word to prayer faithfully. That speaks a lot about us. We don't mind participating in the works of the flesh, but we hesitate or refuse to persist in the walking of the Spirit and mature into perfect sons and daughters of God. Father, I see why You spoke to me about my mouth, for we know full well that I would go off on someone and feel joy in my heart because I had hurt them. But I would also pray. Now I see why the prayers weren't answered, for I had gleefully done wrong and wasn't about to apologize to those offenders. The Spirit of God is so sweet, though. He convicted me of my sins and let me know that I had to bring my life in alignment with the Word of God. I am called to evangelize and to minister and how can I go around calling myself a minister of God when I just continually went around verbally abusing his people? I cannot. He even began to speak to me about things I was saying that weren't even "bad." Then after I was asked to Pastor, I realized why--it was another level and people would be watching me even more. Lifestyle is important. We will be watched. We will be scrutinized--people will look for anything to discredit you! But we are to operate in excellence in all things. We are to have a higher standard than the world. Let us exemplify that in all we do. Not just in word and deed, but in action as well!

Spiritual Attacks

"And they have conquered him by the blood of the Lamb and by the word of their testimony, for they loved not their lives even unto death."

Revelation 12:11

"Evil is an attack against human spiritual development and enlightenment. All evil, badness, neurosis - it has one motive and one motive only, which is to destroy - to destroy your chance of arising above yourself."

Vernon Howard

I was recently visiting a ministry where it was prophesied to me that the devil hated me. That he has always hated me. I often reflect on my childhood and how hard it was for me, then school, then adult life--I used to believe that God hated me! How deceived I was! It was difficult, and I was not trained in the spiritual aspect of life, so I was left bitter and angry. I remember crying in worship services and not knowing why, when it was the Holy Spirit the whole time! No one recognized this? Finally, I was in a place where the believers were taught, and things began to make sense! Wow! I had an enemy who hated me and would try everything he could to disrupt my life and cause me to go to hell.

Satan was trying to get me to go through hell here on earth and then experience it literally after death! And he was focused and determined, and I was unprepared! Then I began to see where he was operating and what he was doing. The Bible says that we are not ignorant of his devices. He is crafty, but I am victorious! God fully equips those who He calls!

I see a lot of attacks going on with the leaders who are determined to teach and preach the Word of God and train up the ministers in the accurate way, totally based on the Word of God. It is usually a vicious attack on their bodies. Pain is usually successful warfare that shuts down the individual. But I see these same individuals going forth in spite of the pain--you will see them limping and in pain but going forth in what they are called to do. This is perseverance! Many would have cancelled and gone to be--and don't get me wrong, be mindful that you need rest and recuperation. Yet, some spiritual attacks come, and you must press forward anyway. You see it for what it is, and you go forth and take care of your business. I pray that the ministries begin to pray wholeheartedly for the leaders, especially the Pastors. The attacks come to take them out of the picture, the very ones who are praying over our souls and our families. I pray that everyone is covered with the Psalm 91 protection and thank God that He is faithful and will complete and perfect that which concerns them. Encourage and strengthen them and surround them with people who will be a blessing to them and not a hindrance. Let us be mature and perfect in Christ and advance the Kingdom!

No!

"Let what you say be simply 'Yes' or 'No'; anything more than this comes from evil."

Matthew 5:7

"I don't like saying 'no' to people, and I'm going to have to learn how to say 'no' more."

Eric Betzig

I am an individual who, if I call myself your friend, then I am going to be just that! I will be with you for years, defending you, encouraging you--even if I need all that myself and you aren't giving it back to me. This buck must stop here. I have allowed so much for so long and now I am exhausted, when if I had set boundaries, I wouldn't be in this predicament! I felt as though people put up with me through my mess and I thought it only right that I do the same. No! There are seasons and steps to process and progress. A baby matures and grows in stages and it can be determined that at certain ages, he should be walking and talking and feeding himself, etc. If a natural baby's growth can be recorded, then we should see progress in the spiritual. If I am somewhere holding a 120-pound baby and feeding it a bottle of formula, there is an issue! It is time for the maturity to take place. One Apostle taught me that she allows someone to come to her twice for advice or counsel and she assists them wholeheartedly. She says when they come the third time, she refuses! I asked her what she told them on the third visit. She responded and said that she had given them the godly instructions and tools to do what they needed and that she was not going any further with it. Immediately, I made up in my mind that I was going to adopt this same solution. I would help someone for years, just knowing that it was going to come to a glorious end! I was in anticipation of the change that was going to come and give the freedom! I was stupid!! I was stuck!! I was stagnant with them!! I was more interested in finding an answer than they were! Chile, you live, and you learn. And I found out that you will lose, too, cause once you say, "No more!" they act as if you betrayed them and then spread lies on you! Go ahead, baby!! Do what you do while I let the Avenger avenge me! I'm good over here!! And it is all about to get even better! I am being set free!!

Silence!

"For God alone, O my soul, wait in silence, for my hope is from him."

Psalm 62:5

"Sometimes you don't have to say anything. Silence speaks it all."
Disha Patani

Why is it that the main ones talking are the ones who are doing the least? I guess that is why they can...they are not doing anything else of any importance. In the life I am living, I don't have time to focus on these other folks, unless I am trying to support them in some fashion. I am one who wants everyone to win! I will do all I can to help you win, but I refuse to watch you as though I am your number one fan. I am busy fulfilling my purpose and it is quite time consuming! Many of the people talking about others have absolutely nothing positive going on in their lives. They are just on the sidelines trying to tell others how to live out their lives. How are you some expert when you are unaccomplished at anything except for running your mouth about the people you need to be like? Just thinking back on it, the very ones trying to tell me what to do are not doing anything at all! Shut up! How can you counsel me, and you are stationary? Get a hold on life and start moving!! Then see me!

Rekindle

"His disciples remembered that it was written, "Zeal for your house will consume me."
John 2:17

"In everyone's life, at some time, our inner fire goes out. It is then burst into flame by an encounter with another human being. We should all be thankful for those people who rekindle the inner spirit."
Albert Schweitzer

I have had to tell myself to get back to the zealous, on fire saint that I used to be. I am presently in love with God, but I am not the fireball I once was. I remember when I first got saved at Shekinah Temple in December of 1990 and I was, at the risk of sounding conceited, AMAZING!! I think back on those days, of the miracles that happened, on the people I met, on the places we went...and I was happy! I was experiencing the Spirit of God like I never knew before, but I knew that this was the God I read of in His Word! It was finally happening before my eyes!

But that isn't the chick of the past few months. I have been so discombobulated...having to encourage myself over and over and it has been exhausting! I made a vow to rekindle my fire when it came to Him. I am going to re-read Good Morning, by Benny

Hinn. That book impacted me in a way that made my life better. I feel better now even just making the decision to do so. I want God in my life like a consuming fire! And I will see Him in all His glory once more!

Form of Religion

"having a form of godliness but denying its power. Have nothing to do with such people."

2 Timothy 3:5

"Religion, in any form, is always interesting to me because of how powerful it is. Not even the religion itself, but to the people that follow it... The effect that it has had on people's minds."

Chino Moreno

I am grieved by how many believers I come in contact with who straight up refuse to follow the commandments given us in the Word of God. There are so many excuses: "I am not perfect;" or "I am not there yet;" or they just flat out refuse. I cannot imagine how this makes the Father feel, the One Who says that they will know us by our love for the brethren. We are not exhibiting love. We are spewing hate and discord and we think we are ok and justified. Therein lies the issue: WE THINK WE ARE OKAY! I hear more Christians quick to talk about telling people off than telling them about the Kingdom. People are quicker to physically fight than to lay holy hands and get rid of these diseases. They are continually talking about someone's downfall and judging them, rather than looking at their own lives and working out their own soul salvation, which would occupy the majority of a day, trust me! My issues are serious! I need the help of the Holy Spirit to keep me in line, and then when I get out of line, I have to repent and get back in the game! Whew! I am a majestic masterpiece, but it is definitely a work in progress! I pray that we become serious about being His Body in the earth, for we are seriously malfunctioning, and we are misrepresenting Him here. He is love and joy and peace. They are looking for Him in us and we are disappointing them greatly, but then we are angered when they say they don't see Him in us, or we don't act accordingly.

Fatigue

"He gives power to the faint, and to him who has no might he increases strength."

Isaiah 40:29

"The first virtue in a soldier is endurance of fatigue; courage is only the second virtue."

Napoleon Bonaparte

There are days where I am just tired...mentally, emotionally, physically and more. It is hard to deal with anything and I don't want to deal with anybody. I feel so heavy in my soul and spirit. I am like a body in molasses, moving slowly and listlessly. I am unable to speak with a lot of these holy Christians for they refuse to simply listen and comfort--they want to do initial sermons or preach revivals and I am just needing to get it all off of me! So, the majority of the time, I just speak with myself and relieve the pressures of life--I seek God of course, but I know that some burdens are my bearing others' burdens. I am grateful to be able to recognize the difference between my weight and other's weights. I do not fully understand the intercessor and all it entails, but I am willing to do what I am called to do.

Healing

"Heal me, O Lord, and I shall be healed; save me, and I shall be saved, for you are my praise."

Jeremiah 17:14

"Healing is a matter of time, but it is sometimes also a matter of opportunity."

Hippocrates

There are times when I am in the process of healing...and it never looks like it. I am still the encouraging, smiling, ministering sister that I always am... but my poor soul can be crying out to God and very few realize it. I thank God that I have a friend that I could go to and release everything that I have holding me down, and she never misses a beat. She is understanding and encouraging herself and she allows me to be me and get it all out without cutting me off or berating me or giving me sermons! I can talk and cry and be comforted and uplifted. This is the great thing about a great friend. You can be you and not be judged. My heart is broken sometimes from people--and I really hate this part, for I didn't want to be around people anyways, but...here we are! (I am literally laughing at that part!) I hate that I even care that much.

119

God truly changes a person, for I used to wish people to hell and wait for them to die. Now I love them so much that I cannot even think of doing to them what I would have gladly done to them before I received salvation. I may not show the effects of my pain, or even react publicly to others when they do hurt me, but it cuts deeply, especially with those you poured into and then they flip on you like a world class gymnast! My prayer is that God show me how to love like He does and to keeps me that I may not become bitter and angry. I know the Word and I plan to live it to the fullest! So, I will be healed and set free and my God will teach me how to walk worthy of the calling and this shall not affect me as it has been.

Awakening

"For anything that becomes visible is light. Therefore, it says, "Awake, O sleeper, and arise from the dead, and Christ will shine on you."

Ephesians 5:14

"If you love God, you can't hate anything or anyone. If the love one offers is met with hate, it doesn't die, rather it manifests in the form of compassion. That is universal love. It is not just a sentiment. It cannot be manifested merely by a shift in mental disposition. It can only come from inner cleaning, an inner awakening."

Radhanath Swami

Generally, when I awaken, it isn't a beautiful picture.... I am grouchy and dragging and sometimes as I begin to speak to the Lord, I don't sound grateful--definitely don't look like it! It takes me a good minute to get into the groove, but once I do, it is on and poppin'!!!!! I know that a Christian has the joy of the Lord, but I am not always experiencing it!! That is when I begin to speak to myself out loud to stir myself up in the spirit so I can operate in the natural. I sit and try to imagine how it must have felt in Eden, not having to deal with any negative feelings but just enjoying the fellowship with the Lord of all the earth...I know it was phenomenal and I cannot wait to experience it for myself!! I feel the Spirit sometimes so heavily that I feel as though I am going to leave my body! I was on the Zoom app with the mentorship class and remembered a time when my spirit hovered over my boy while

I was doing praise and worship after just getting saved! It was like nothing I have ever known! I was I looking down at my body singing and praising God. Of course, I didn't ask anyone anything about it, because I never heard anyone talk about it! But as you learn more about the things of God, so much more is clarified! I want to awaken more to the things of the Spirit, as well as awakening each morning with expectancy and joy.

Understanding

"A fool takes no pleasure in understanding, but only in expressing his opinion."

Proverbs 18:2

"If people are going to judge me without fully understanding the content of my character, then their opinion just isn't worth it."

Jazz Jennings

It angers me when I am trying to convey a thought or feeling and the person who is supposed to be listening is constantly interrupting or trying to counsel me before I am done. I understand that you have something to say, and I obviously think enough of you to come to you and seek your counsel, so please just SHUT UP FOR A MINUTE! I tell my son often that I miss the old Stephanie sometimes because she freely said what she felt, regardless of how it made others feel. I was not weighted down with concern for hurt feelings or anything of that sort. Now my speech is to be seasoned with grace, but I must get to the place where I allow the Holy Spirit to put the season on, because I can take it to the level where it should not be! I am maturing in this area. I need to grow more in the area of the tongue. And evidently, so do others! (I laughed inside myself while I typed this!) We all need to watch our mouths...some to use it less or better, and others need to use it more and louder. It is interesting to see where we all are when it comes to the tongue. I just want to be pleasing to God. And, man, is it an adventurous walk!!!

Honor

"Honor everyone. Love the brotherhood. Fear God. Honor the emperor."

1 Peter 2:17

"You will never do anything in this world without courage. It is the greatest quality of the mind next to honor."

Aristotle

I was asked to do spoken word at a seminar. This young lady is such an inspiration to me, and I was honored to be asked. I tried for a month to get my piece right...I began to be frustrated as the time grew closer and I still didn't have my piece completed. I knew about the theme and I knew I was blessed with the gift to write poetry. But when I tell you that I would be rehearsing, and I would be stuttering and couldn't get the words out! I was feeling crazy! I finally asked the Lord what was going on, because it was not coming together as I wanted it to. Then, He began to give me what I was to write, and I felt the Spirit fall on me. I began to get excited and quickly began typing. It brought tears to my eyes as I completed it. I took it, printed it, and put it in a frame. At the Purpose seminar, I read it to her, for it was a piece that honored her. Give the flowers while they can still smell them.

Reconciliation

"Therefore, if you are offering your gift at the altar and there remember that your brother or sister has something against you, leave your gift there in front of the altar. First go and be reconciled to them; then come and offer your gift."
Matthew 5:23, 24

"Reconciliation is a part of the healing process, but how can there be healing when the wounds are still being inflicted?"
N. K. Jemisin

I am a sister that likes to clear the air. In the past, if I heard that someone had an issue with me, but never said anything to me, but continued to smile and laugh and chat with me as if there was nothing wrong, I would go to them. The majority of the time, the party would deny that there was an issue, even though their body language said otherwise, and I already knew because it had been relayed to me prior to my asking. If it was confessed that they had an issue, they would try to say that I was the one who caused the bad feelings, but if that were so, then why did they not come to me, as I had to them? Why did you go to someone else and tell them so plainly what you should have been telling me? Well, I found out later through a number of people that I am "hard to approach" when it comes to trying to speak with me. I'm not denying it-- obviously it has to be true, since so few are taking the time to do so when they need to speak with me. So, what am I doing wrong? I still am praying about that, for I need to correct that and be the person that others can come to and feel free to have a conversation with and voice their displeasure. But I feel great pleasure when I do encounter the few who reach out to me to speak their minds. I know that I can be domineering and overbearing. I need to work on that. I find that I am often overlooked or ignored, and I become belligerent in order to be heard because the other party doesn't see the value in my words and I WILL BE HEARD! I am a great fan of reconciliation. Coming together to talk things out is a big one.

Disappointments

"Let not your heart envy sinners, but continue in the fear of
the Lord all the day. Surely there is a future, and your hope will not
be cut off."
Proverbs 23:17-18

"Depression begins with disappointment. When disappointment
festers in our soul, it leads to discouragement."
Joyce Meyer

I was surprised in so many ways about this walk with Christ. I thought that the ones who were down with me would always be down and the ones who weren't would keep their distance. It was totally unexpected to witness people walk away from me without a backwards glance and to see people step into place who God had brought strategically to me to assist me in this walk of victory. Sometimes I didn't even realize how much I needed the encouragement until I was on the phone with the special ones He sent. But on this journey, there is a continual shifting in the relationships and it is painful, but I know that if God is doing it, then it is necessary.

Small Things

"and after the earthquake a fire, *but* the Lord *was* not in the fire;
and after the fire a still small voice."
1 Kings 19:12

"My hope for my children must be that they respond to the still,
small voice of God in their own hearts."
Andrew Young

I have noticed that the Lord has increased His speaking to me.
It will be small nudges that lead me and guide me throughout the
day. It will be something as simple as not to put gum in my mouth
before I get on a live session on Facebook. I disregarded it and
ended up looking like a cow chewing a cud when we were doing
the live! I was laughing at myself as I watched the video replay. I
am so hardheaded sometimes when it comes to stuff like that! The
Spirit was so gently speaking and just as gently I ignored Him! I
cannot remember the other incidents that happened, too, but I do
know that it was Him trying to assist me in my everyday life! I am
grateful for Him and I must learn to immediately do what He is
asking me to do. I know that I will be engaged with Him in
conversation but often when directed to do something, I will either
hesitate or I will try to analyze it before I obey. And I remember
hearing that delayed obedience is disobedience. Even though I

eventually go and complete the task, I should not have argued or questioned or delayed when the directive came forth. I appreciate the growth that occurred with Him. I still need to go deeper in Him, for I feel Him calling me. And I will go further in Him.

Cup of Tea

"The person without the Spirit does not accept the things that come from the Spirit of God but considers them foolishness, and cannot understand them because they are discerned only through the Spirit."
1 Corinthians 2:14

"We need discernment in what we see and what we hear and what we believe."
Charles R. Swindoll

Everyone is not my cup of tea. And that is just fine with me. A lot of people are trying to get me to be a part of something with people that I know full well that my spirit is not clicking with and I refuse. Why test the spirit by the Spirit if once He lets me know that they are poisonous, I am going to be foolish to still go and get poisoned? No ma'am! That's stupidity and I will not do it. Some people I cannot even deal with hearing their voice, because instead of hearing their voices I hear the demons growling. I have done enough in my life and I don't plan to keep making the mistakes. I will bless the Lord without you in my circle and you can do whatever you are doing in your arena. I am not the type to keep someone else from mingling with whomever they choose, just know that I have made my stance known. And I would appreciate it if you accepted it the same way that I accepted your decision you made to choose to speak to them and be a part of that circle. We are good either way. That has no bearing on our relationship unless you allow it to. Just as I am not everyone's cup of tea. There are people who would not desire to be in my presence. And that is fantastic, for we have the freedom to make that choice! The sun will still rise and set, and our lives will still continue to go forth! Fret not! We need not bother to have any ill will. It is what it is and I am okay with it. Trying to force me to talk with or be around someone that I don't wish to be is only going to cause you more issues than me, because I will back away from you since your respect for my decision is missing. Just let me be. Go forth and enjoy them and your life! Much love and peace.

Submission

[22] "Wives, submit to your own husbands, as to the Lord. [23] For the husband is head of the wife, as also Christ is head of the church; and He is the Savior of the body."

Ephesians 5:22-23

"I do not make any apologies for my manner or personality. I come from a long line of very strong, black African American women who neither bend nor bow. I haven't had very good modeling in submission."

Faye Wattleton

It is difficult for me to submit to my husband. I am so used to being in control and doing my own thing, and being independent, that is taking some getting used to. I am not saying that I will not be submissive. I am saying that it is difficult. I have been doing things on my own for years. I wasn't in a lot of significant relationships. I was a whore, so I was just sleeping around. I didn't want a man to linger after the childhood I had--I didn't think that I was lovable, so I would not let too many people get too close, lest they see the unlovable parts of me. I still to this day laugh at my husband, telling him, "You're crazy! I love me and I would not have married me!" I know that I am a whole handful. There are times I get on my own nerves! Now what do you do when you cannot get away from yourself? Better learn how to deal! I hear the women saying you have to do this for your husband or that for your husband...and I am thinking, "What?" One thing is that Carlos Rice knew me for eight years before he married me. So, he was fully aware of the crazy chick that he was marrying! He knew I was not the cook of the family--he is amazing in that area. He knew that I was out and about doing events in the community--he is just as busy, coaching various events in the community. I just want to be great in my own arena, and I found out that what works for others won't always be the success you are looking for. You as husband and wife know each other and what works for you is what you should do. I listen when people are giving me instruction, but I also know what to apply and what to discard as inapplicable to me and mine. But I am growing in Christ still and I will be more submissive to this man I have married.

Carnality

"For ye are yet carnal: for whereas [there is] among you envying, and strife, and divisions, are ye not carnal, and walk as men?"
1 Corinthians 3:3

"The carnal nature of man is that he places his tribe above others, but the only basis for the power and unity of the church is that there is no Jew or Gentile."
Yemi Osinbajo

I am amazed at the apathy, the indifference from people, not just the people of God, but people in general. There are things going on in the world that we should be taking a stand against, or not participating in at all, but we are taking the time to talk about it while we do nothing, or participate in mess that has nothing to do with us or our well-being. I see the posts about places around the world without clean drinking water or babies being kidnapped and killed, but we are still focused on the irrelevant issues that govern the news or social media. I know that God's people should have the heart of God, but it seems as if our hearts are hardened and we sit uncaringly and watch as all the evil goes down and won't even lift up a prayer to get God Himself on the scene! We are not to be seated comfortably in our homes and discussing on Facebook the popular topics at that time. We are to be coming against anything that is not of Christ! You cannot even have an intelligent conversation with a fellow believer because he is so caught up with the earthly mess going on that we aren't tuned in with the spiritual realm where the answers are! We have the answers--a lot of us are answers to the problems going on, but we are not willing to be the solution! I thank God that I am listening for His voice and following His leading and being a change in the earth that I want to see! We are to affect the world, not have it affect us!

Enemies

"For the LORD your God is the one who goes with you to fight for you against your enemies to give you victory."

Deuteronomy 20:4

Real men laugh at opposition; real men smile when enemies appear.

Marcus Garvey

I remember the Scripture that Jesus spoke of which speaks of enemies being of one's own household. It grieves me as I see facebook posts about the issues with family members and bothers me even more when they begin to argue on facebook for the whole world to see and everyone starts commenting on it and taking sides and adding their two cents in. The family shouldn't even be arguing on social media, so you definitely shouldn't be adding to the confusion! What is wrong with people? Now, granted, it is social media. And I agree that everyone has the right to post what they wish on their page. I am just saying that there are those who are rejoicing in the fact that you are fighting and some of them are egging it on with their comments. I hate it even more that my advice to those arguing would be to just not speak to each other. Let it be and live your life. It does no good to be going back and forth and everyone is angry, but nothing gets fixed at all. Now I also understand that some people like the drama and the anger. I was one who felt as though the anger was fueling my life, not blood in my veins. It is sad that most of the times the dysfunctional habits are learned early in childhood and we carry them throughout our lives and pass them down to generations. I passed down anger to Stephano unknowingly and when he unleashed his, he was something to be reckoned with! I was like, WHOA! And I was dismayed to know that I had given him that part of me, when I could have dealt with that and did so much better! So, I just spoke with him and we spoke of generational curses and I apologized to him about not realizing that I had cursed him with anger. Just seeing him deal with it sometimes bothers me. But I didn't know and couldn't help him because I didn't even help myself until I was in my 40s. I pray for him and I continue to pray for myself for we are victorious--I don't care what it looks like!

ABOUT THE AUTHOR

Stephanie Johnson-Rice is the wife of Carlos Rice and the mother of one son Stephano Derrell Arnez Johnson. She is a pastor, entrepreneur, poet, comedian, and emcee/host amongst a list of other great gifts she has had bestowed upon her! She likes to call herself a Peculiar Princess, who is Unleashing Uniqueness to the Universe, as she walks her own path that was prepared for her.